IT IS FINISHED

I will cause you to walk in My ways and I will plant My fear in your heart. I know you cannot do this for yourself, but don't worry—I will do it all for you, with your cooperation. This work is accomplished only by faith in the finished work of the cross. All I ask is that you trust My promises to you. The work has already been accomplished by Me. It is your work to accept it by faith. That is My everlasting covenant.

DISCUSSION QUESTIONS

1. Psalm 21:3 uses the unusual phrase, "Thou preventest him." What does the word *preventest* mean in the original language? (Page 173)

2. The second part of Psalm 21:3 says, "Thou settest a crown of pure gold on his head." What does the gold crown symbolize? How does this passage apply to us? (Page 179)

3. God has anticipated all our struggles and our battles with sin, the flesh and the devil. In His mercy and goodness, what has He done for us? (Page 179)

4. How does the Holy Spirit drive out fear? (Page 180)

5. Many struggle to live in God's covenant promises because of a lack of two things. What are they? What is a key Scripture to understanding this truth? (Pages 180–181)

6. When did God forgive King David for his sin of adultery and all the sins that followed? (Page 182)

7. The parable of the Prodigal Son is a wonderful example of our heavenly Father's willingness to forgive His wayward child (see Luke 15). When was the Prodigal forgiven? (Page 186)

8. The way to cleansing and restoration is by what? (Page 186)

9. In your own words, summarize what the covenant promises mean to you.

The Rev. David Wilkerson was perhaps best known for his early days of ministry to young drug addicts and gang members in New York City. His story is told in *The Cross and the Switchblade*, a book he co-authored in 1962 that has been read by more than fifteen million people in some thirty languages. The story was made into a Hollywood motion picture in 1970.

Rev. Wilkerson served as pastor in small churches in Pennsylvania until 1958, when he saw a photograph in *Life* magazine of several New York City teenagers charged with murder. Moved with compassion, he was drawn to the city and began a street ministry to what one writer called "desperate, bewildered, addicted, often violent youth." A year later, Rev. Wilkerson founded Teen Challenge in Brooklyn, which today reaches youth and adults with life-controlling problems through almost twelve hundred centers in 91 countries.

Working under his global ministry, World Challenge, Inc., Rev. Wilkerson conducted evangelistic crusades and pastors' conferences, produced films, authored more than thirty books, including his recent *God Is Faithful*, and instituted feeding programs—which continue to this day—in some of the world's poorest areas.

In 1987, he founded Times Square Church in New York City. Today, the mission-focused congregation includes more than eight thousand people representing more than one hundred nationalities.

On April 27, 2011, Rev. Wilkerson posted this on his devotional blog: "To those going through the valley and shadow of death, hear this word: Weeping will last through some dark, awful nights, and in that darkness you will soon hear the Father whisper, 'I am with you. I cannot tell you why right now, but one day it will make sense. You will see it was all part of My plan. It was no accident.'" That afternoon, Rev. Wilkerson was killed in a car crash. His wife, Gwen, died on July 5, 2012. They are survived by their four children and their spouses, ten grandchildren and two great-grandchildren.

To learn more about David Wilkerson's ongoing ministry, go to http://www.worldchallenge.org.

To read more of David Wilkerson's daily devotions, you may go to http://davidwilkersontoday.blogspot.com/.

IT *IS*
FINISHED

FINDING LASTING VICTORY
Over SIN

DAVID WILKERSON

Chosen
a division of Baker Publishing Group
Minneapolis, Minnesota

Previously published under the title *The New Covenant Unveiled*

Published by Chosen Books
11400 Hampshire Avenue South
Bloomington, Minnesota 55438
www.chosenbooks.com

Chosen Books is a division of
Baker Publishing Group, Grand Rapids, Michigan

Printed in the United States of America

Library of Congress Cataloging-in-Publication Data
Wilkerson, David, 1931–2011.
    It is finished : finding lasting victory over sin / David Wilkerson.
      p. cm.
    Rev. ed. of: The new covenant unveiled. c2000.
    Summary: "The founder of Teen Challenge and author of The Cross and the Switchblade reveals the key to truly defeating persistent sins and life-draining, life-controlling bondage"—Provided by publisher.
    ISBN 978-0-8007-9574-0 (cloth : alk. paper)
    ISBN 978-0-8007-9549-8 (pbk. : alk. paper)
    1. Covenants—Religious aspects—Christianity—Sermons. 2. Sermons, American. I. Wilkerson, David, 1931–2011. New covenant unveiled. II. Title.
BT155.W58 2013
248.4—dc23   2012042337

In keeping with biblical principles of creation stewardship, Baker Publishing Group advocates the responsible use of our natural resources. As a member of the Green Press Initiative, our company uses recycled paper when possible. The text paper of this book is composed in part of post-consumer waste.

Cover design by Gearbox

13   14   15   16   17   18   19   7   6   5   4   3   2   1

CONTENTS

CONTENTS

FOREWORD

On the day my father died, he spent his last morning on a porch studying the New Covenant of Christ. The subject was by no means new to him. Twenty-five years earlier, his good friend Leonard Ravenhill had given him a few books that would change his life. At that time, my father was busy traveling the world as an evangelist, preaching to hundreds of thousands each year. Yet his own soul was dry; he had become weary of preaching the same messages again and again. So between those trips he picked up the small stack of books Leonard had handed him and started reading.

They were the writings of the old Puritans—names most of us have never heard of, certainly not the familiar bestselling authors many Christians have read. As my father dug into these old treasures, his heart opened to a new revelation of Christ. Grace awakened in him, alive in a way he had never known.

Dad had grown up under a message that leaned toward works and legalism. Although he considered himself free in Christ, there was still something in him that made him feel as though he had to work hard—that nothing was ever enough, that more was always required to fill what was missing in his righteousness in Christ. These old books stirred him once again to study the

Scriptures cover to cover, this time with a new understanding of the Gospel. As he explored, my father joyously came to know the full extent of the finished work of Christ.

In my last conversation with him, Dad told me of how deeply he had probed, how fully he had explored, how completely he had scoured every page of every writing he could find on this glorious subject of the New Covenant of Christ. And yet I could see in his eyes there was a yearning for more. There were still many things he wanted to know concerning the depth and breadth of the finished work of Christ. He felt he had seen and learned much, but he urged me to dig deeper in my own study of this subject—not to be satisfied but to go further.

A few weeks after my father's funeral, my brother-in-law sent me the book Dad had been reading that last morning. It was by the Puritan writer Thomas Brooks. Almost every page was underlined and highlighted, with comments filling every open margin. Here was my father, eighty years old—after seven decades of serving in ministry—still exploring, still enjoying, still reveling in the glorious Gospel of Christ. He relished the revelation of how expansive Jesus' words are when He declares from the cross, "It is finished." Jesus was speaking not only of the work He did for us then, but also of the work He continues to do in us and through us today.

I hope you will explore and even devour this book—that you will find in it the richest depths of meaning in Christ's words: *It is finished*. Here is God's great love contained in His marvelous New Covenant. As you read these pages, may you be stirred to underline, highlight and write in the margins every revelation Jesus longs for you to know, experience and enjoy of His finished work for you.

Gary Wilkerson
Colorado Springs, 2012

INTRODUCTION

The Body of Jesus Christ today desperately needs a fresh unveiling of God's New Covenant. We need it because our generation is living in a time of powerful demonic seductions. Jesus warned that such days would come—days in which Satan would attempt to deceive even the elect of God. Today we are seeing Jesus' words come to pass, as humankind faces an overwhelming flood of temptations unknown to any past generation.

The devil appears to have taken control of much of the media. Less than a century ago, there was no such thing as television, the Internet or videos. The airwaves were not polluted then, but today the atmosphere is saturated with devilish filth, as satellites beam pornography to homes all over the world. The technological advances meant to improve our lives have opened wide the floodgates of evil, and society is being inundated by seductions that are coming upon us with a ferocity we have never seen. Satan is using virtually every form of media to feed dormant lusts, encourage promiscuity and destroy every semblance of morality. In the process he is breaking up homes and marriages.

Tragically, many Christians are being swept up in this demonic web of sensuality. Believers who have flirted with secret sins

9

now find themselves in a battle for their souls. Our ministry receives thousands of letters each week, many from distraught believers who describe being trapped in sinful bondages. They tell us of life-controlling habits in their own lives and in the lives of loved ones—habits such as drugs, alcohol, smoking, pornography, adultery, fornication, homosexuality, gambling, bitterness, anger, covetousness and stealing. Yet, no matter what their struggle, all of these people have this in common: They are bound, snared in slavery by a besetting sin. They feel chained, unable to break free from sin's power.

Many of these dear people sincerely love Jesus. They have prayed diligently, cried a river of tears and sought counseling from pastors and friends, yet nothing seems to free them. They always end up going back to their sin, and their heavy burden of guilt only increases with time.

Many such Christians have concluded they can never be free from their sin. They think they will never be able to move out of the bondage of flesh Paul describes in Romans 7. In this bondage, Paul says, a person does what he hates, with no power to do what is right. He is unable to move into the spiritual freedom Paul outlines so joyously in Romans 8, where power over the dominion of sin is revealed. In the bound person's eyes, there is no escape from the wretchedness of always doing what he despises. So he has resigned himself to struggling for the rest of his life—riding the unending merry-go-round of sinning and confessing, sinning and confessing. Yet, all the while, he continues to testify of God's power to set others free.

The New Covenant has nothing to offer those who are at peace with their sin—but it promises great hope to those who hate their sin. If you are a believer who hates your sin—if you still grieve over your bondage to a habitual lust; if you cry out to the Lord to deliver you from Satan's snare; if you feel helpless, weak, despondent over your lack of power—I have good news for you. The New Covenant provides for your absolute freedom. Our Lord has made available to you not only pardon for all sin and its guilt, but also liberty from and dominion over all bondage. These wonderful things are available to you through the glorious provisions of the New Covenant.

The provisions of the New Covenant set us free from the power of sin and deliver us into the Spirit of life. We do not have to do the devil's bidding anymore, because by covenant God has promised to empower us to win over all temptations and lusts. All indwelling sin can be stripped of its dominion through the power of the indwelling Holy Spirit.

In my later years, I have concluded that laying hold of the New Covenant is the only way to break free from the power and dominion of sin. I hope to show you in this book how that glorious work takes place. Yet the unveiling of the New Covenant is not something within my power or ability to do. Only the Holy Spirit can open up its marvelous truths to the seeker. I can, however, assure all who are discouraged by their lack of victory over a besetting sin that this book can open your eyes to the incredible promises and provisions God has given to all who intensely yearn for freedom from sin's dominion. May the Holy Spirit unveil the glory and power of the New Covenant to every seeker who desires to walk in holiness and peace.

This book is composed of messages preached at Times Square Church in New York City. Because of this, you will find certain basic covenant truths repeated throughout the book (and portions italicized for emphasis), in an effort to imprint them firmly in your heart and mind. I pray the Lord will use these messages to bring hope and knowledge to you concerning His commitment to keep and deliver His people from the dominion of sin.

David Wilkerson

1

UNDERSTANDING
THE NEW COVENANT

"My covenant I will not break, nor alter the word that has gone out of My lips" (Psalm 89:34).

What is God talking about, exactly, when He speaks of covenant? *Covenant* is "an agreement or pledge between two or more parties." Today we would use the word *contract* to describe a covenant. And like any contract, a covenant contains terms or duties that each party has to perform in order to fulfill the agreement. Such covenants are legally binding and once they have been finalized, the parties can be penalized for not fulfilling their respective terms.

The term *covenant* plays an integral part in the Christian faith. The Holy Scriptures themselves are divided into an Old Covenant (or Testament) and a New Covenant. I believe it is vitally important for the Church of Jesus Christ to comprehend the New Covenant as we face the coming perilous times. The

Bible tells us that in the last days Satan is going to pour out his wrath on the earth because he knows his time is short. As that happens, God's people are going to need the full assurance of this covenant. This ironclad pledge has the power to release in all of us the overcoming strength we need to be more than conquerors in any situation.

When I was a young Christian, I was led to believe that covenant theology was a licentious doctrine taught by a few dying religious groups. The thinking then seemed to be that the New Covenant is so marvelously freeing, people could take advantage of it and misuse it. It was seen as a teaching that could lead to a permissive, compromising lifestyle.

Others have wrongly taught that the New Covenant is God's pledge to baptize His people with financial bonanzas—expensive cars, grand houses, material wealth, immunity to sorrow and sickness. These teachers have completely perverted God's glorious covenant and reduced it to that which ministers only to man's greed.

In spite of all this, the more I understand about the New Covenant, the more I am convinced that it is meant for us today. More importantly, I believe it is the one truth that can release in us God's supernatural power to overcome in these last days.

Unclaimed Promises

The book of Hebrews, which refers to the New Covenant at length, provides this description:

> "Behold, the days are coming, says the LORD, when I will make a new covenant with the house of Israel and with the house of Judah—not according to the covenant that I made with their

fathers in the day when I took them by the hand to lead them out of the land of Egypt; because they did not continue in My covenant, and I disregarded them, says the LORD.

"For this is the covenant that I will make with the house of Israel after those days, says the LORD: I will put My laws in their mind and write them on their hearts; and I will be their God, and they shall be My people. None of them shall teach his neighbor, and none his brother, saying, 'Know the LORD,' for all shall know Me, from the least of them to the greatest of them. For I will be merciful to their unrighteousness, and their sins and their lawless deeds I will remember no more."

In that He says, "A new covenant," He has made the first obsolete. Now what is becoming obsolete and growing old is ready to vanish away.

Hebrews 8:8–13

"This is the covenant that I will make with them after those days, says the LORD: I will put My laws into their hearts, and in their minds I will write them," then He adds, "Their sins and their lawless deeds I will remember no more."

Hebrews 10:16–17

This summary details the eternal promises of God's incredible New Covenant. So, why is this wonderful truth unsought or ignored by Christians today?

I believe the passage itself provides a key to this oversight. It describes "a new covenant with the house of Israel and with the house of Judah" (Hebrews 8:8). Many Christian groups have mistaken this verse to mean that the New Covenant applies only to natural Jews, rather than to the spiritual Jews who make up Christ's Body. Modern dispensationalists, for example, interpret this verse as a promise meant only for literal Israel. So they assign its meaning to a coming millennial age.

It is no wonder the New Covenant has remained unclaimed for so long. Yet the truth is, all these promises of the New Covenant are yours and mine, right now. They are for all believing Jews and Gentiles. How do I know this? It is clear from the context of the above passage that the house of Israel refers to spiritual Israel, meaning all who are in Jesus Christ.

"Natural" Israel and "Spiritual" Israel

The word *Israel* itself, as first used in Genesis 32:28, is filled with spiritual meaning: "And He said, 'Your name shall no longer be called Jacob, but Israel; for you have struggled with God and with men, and have prevailed.'" *Israel* was Jacob's regenerate name. It was given to him by God after his carnal spirit was broken and his nature was changed.

In many Bible passages, of course, the word *Israel* refers to Jacob's natural descendants. In others it points to God's spiritual seed. One example of the latter is Psalm 73:1: "Truly God is good to Israel, to such as are pure in heart." Here the psalmist is speaking prophetically, distinguishing Israel as people whose hearts have been cleansed—which is possible only through the blood of Christ. The Old Covenant sacrificial system could not cleanse the conscience:

> It was symbolic for the present time in which both gifts and sacrifices are offered which cannot make him who performed the service perfect in regard to the conscience—concerned only with foods and drinks, various washings, and fleshly ordinances.
>
> Hebrews 9:9–10

The apostle Paul also speaks of Israel as God's spiritual seed. Throughout the New Testament, he distinguishes between two kinds of Israel, one natural and one spiritual. Paul emphasizes that it is not the natural Jew but the person who puts his faith in Jesus Christ who becomes Abraham's spiritual seed:

- "They are not all Israel who are of Israel" (Romans 9:6).
- "Therefore know that only those who are of faith are sons of Abraham" (Galatians 3:7).
- "Those who are the children of the flesh, these are not the children of God; but the children of the promise are counted as the seed" (Romans 9:8).
- "He is not a Jew who is one outwardly, nor is circumcision that which is outward in the flesh; but he is a Jew who is one inwardly; and circumcision is that of the heart, in the Spirit, not in the letter; whose praise is not from men but from God" (Romans 2:28–29).
- "This Hagar is Mount Sinai in Arabia, and corresponds to Jerusalem which now is, and is in bondage with her children—but the Jerusalem above is free, which is the mother of us all" (Galatians 4:25–26).

It is clear from these passages that there is a spiritual Israel as well as a natural Israel. Moreover, Scripture reveals that God, through Christ, made His New Covenant with spiritual Israel. The writer of Hebrews says, "Now He has obtained a more excellent ministry, inasmuch as He is also Mediator of a better covenant, which was established on better promises" (Hebrews 8:6).

Am I saying the Lord is finished with natural Israel? God forbid. Many Christians today do not wish to see God's hand moving on natural Israel to fulfill her prophetic role. Yet it was the Jewish people who received the promises and covenants of the Old Testament. In the past sixty generations, we have seen storms arise against this people. Time after time, conquerors have sought to annihilate them. Mobs have set in for the kill. Dictators incarnated by Satan have attempted to wipe out the very history of the Jews. But all these enemies have risen up against them to no avail.

I believe that the national revival of the state of Israel, and the many supernatural deliverances of that nation, point to an infinitely deep mystery revealing the very hand of God. God still loves the Jews. One day the veil will be removed from Israel, and a remnant, a part of her people, will acknowledge Christ as Lord.

I stand with Paul, who wrote, "They are beloved for the sake of the fathers" (Romans 11:28). "Has God cast away His people? Certainly not! For I also am an Israelite. . . . Even so then, at this present time there is a remnant according to the election of grace" (Romans 11:1, 5). The Church has not replaced Israel. It includes both Gentiles and believing Jews.

This New Covenant, however, was not meant for natural Israel—not then, not now, nor in some millennial period. It is meant for spiritual Israel, meaning every Jew and Gentile who is born again in Jesus. It is for repentant believers in Christ alone.

THE TERMS OF THE NEW COVENANT

With whom did God make this covenant? And what are its terms?

God cut it with His Son, Jesus—and they agreed to its terms before the very foundation of the world. Paul spoke of "eternal life which God, who cannot lie, promised [covenanted] before time [the world, KJV] began" (Titus 1:2). Paul also said that God "saved us and called us . . . according to His own purpose and grace which was given to us in Christ Jesus before time began" (2 Timothy 1:9).

This covenant was a formal agreement between Father and Son. And today we, the seed of spiritual Israel, are brought into this covenant by faith. In other words, since we are one with Christ through faith, the covenant was cut with us also.

Amazingly, this heavenly contract work was not done in secret. The Bible openly records the terms. As we examine these covenant arrangements, it becomes clear that God wants us to be encouraged by such a detailed revelation.

The Father's Purpose in the Covenant

Psalm 89:19 gives us a snapshot of the discourse between Father and Son: "You spoke in a vision to Your holy one, and said: 'I have given help to one who is mighty; I have exalted one chosen from the people.'"

The Father was saying to His Son, "This is a mysterious word I am about to give You. Humankind is going to grow weak and miserable because of their sin. They will become overwhelmed, helpless to find their way back to Me. So I am appointing You as My Holy One to help them. I am sending You to them as one mightier than they, to bring them back into My favor."

Here, in simple terms, is God's primary purpose in formulating the New Covenant. *It was to recover a lost humanity from the devil's power.* The heavenly Father was not willing to lose His beloved creation to the powers of hell, so He formed a redemption plan—one that came completely from His heart of love, before the world was created.

Jesus Accepts the Terms

Next, we hear the Son's covenant agreements: "Behold, I come; in the scroll of the book it is written of me. I delight to do Your will, O my God, and Your law is within my heart" (Psalm 40:7–8).

Jesus answered the Father this way: "You have shown Me that Your help to humanity is going to be laid upon My shoulders. You are sending Me to rescue the imprisoned, heal the hurting, break satanic strongholds and reconcile creation back to You. Father, I accept this charge to take on the redemption of the lost, and I accept the might and power You will give Me to accomplish the task."

God then laid out before His Son the type of ministry He would have to undertake in order to redeem humankind. He told Jesus, "Your ministry is going to be that of a priest and shepherd to My children. They will be Your flock, and You will be a shepherd to them. You will lead them beside still waters and into green pastures. You will walk with them through every shadow of death. And if any one of them ever goes astray, You will take him in Your arms and bring him back to My love. You will restore his soul and bring him great comfort."

We know from the Bible that Jesus kept all of these terms of the covenant. And He continues to give special attention to every single sheep in His care: "He calls his own sheep by name" (John 10:3). Further, He says, "All that the Father gives Me will come to Me, and the one who comes to Me I will by no means cast out. For I have come down from heaven, not to do My own will, but the will of Him who sent Me" (John 6:37–38).

Finally, the Father gave His Son these instructions: "As You go to earth for Me—since You have agreed to seek out My lost ones—these works will be required of You:

"You must preach good tidings to the meek . . . bind up the brokenhearted . . . proclaim liberty to the captives . . . open prison doors to all who are bound . . . bear with the weaknesses of the frail . . . break not a bruised reed . . . quench not a smoking flame . . . bear tenderly with the ignorant . . . feed the flock . . . supply their shortcomings with Your strength . . . gather all the lambs into Your arms and carry them in Your bosom . . . gently lead the young . . . lend Your strength to the weak . . . guide them with Your counsel . . . promise to send them the Holy Spirit to carry on the work of freedom . . . cherish them, perfect them and bring them home to glory with You."

Later, when Jesus lived on earth, He testified, "My food is to do the will of Him who sent Me, and to finish His work" (John 4:34). Everything Christ did on earth was in fulfillment of the covenant terms He had made with His Father. His every word and deed reflected what they had agreed upon before the world came into being. And their agreement included this incredible term: "This command I have received from my Father . . . [to] lay down My life" (John 10:18, 17).

What the Father Gave in Return

God gave His Son these everlasting covenant promises:

- "You will have the Holy Spirit upon You without measure." Jesus testified, "The Spirit of the Lord GOD is upon Me" (Isaiah 61:1). Christ did not have just a small portion of the Spirit, coming to Him in little drops. He had the Father's Spirit in fullness, without measure: "For God does not give the Spirit by measure" (John 3:34).

- "You will never be out of My sight. My presence will always be with You." According to the author of Hebrews, God gave this promise to Jesus: "I will be to Him a Father, and He shall be to Me a Son" (Hebrews 1:5). This meant Christ would constantly be under His Father's watchful eye. He would always have the Father's help available to Him.

- "I will lift You up in all times of opposition and discouragement." Isaiah wrote: "He will not fail nor be discouraged, till He has established justice in the earth; and the coast-lands shall wait for His law" (Isaiah 42:4). God is saying, "Every time the enemy brings discouragement upon You, I will be there to counteract it. I'm going to encourage You by My Spirit every time You need it."

- "I will highly exalt You and give You a name above all other names." Paul wrote, "God also has highly exalted Him and given Him the name which is above every name, that at the name of Jesus every knee should bow" (Philippians 2:9–10).

- "After Your work is finished, I will bring You back to glory." Jesus said, "Ought not the Christ to have suffered these things and to enter into His glory?" (Luke 24:26). He knew the Father had promised, "Son, after You have fulfilled all the terms of the covenant, I will bring You back to glory—in victory, power and anointing."

The Father made this covenant pledge to His Son: "I, the LORD, have called You in righteousness, and will hold Your hand; I will keep You and give You as a covenant to the people, as a light to the Gentiles" (Isaiah 42:6). God was saying, "My hand will always be holding on to Yours. You will never be away from My keeping power. I pledge to keep You safe from all the schemes of the devil."

And Christ appropriated this promise of help from His Father: "My God shall be My strength" (Isaiah 49:5), and "I will put My trust in Him" (Hebrews 2:13). He was saying in these verses, "My Father made a covenant with Me, and it's settled. It is good for eternity, because He cannot lie. He said He would be My strength—and now I appropriate all of that promised power."

Here are all the terms of the covenant, laid out in black and white for every believer to see. The Father and Son have hidden none of them from us. They want us to be encouraged by them all. The Father is showing us His faithfulness to His Son, to prove to us He will be just as faithful to us, Christ's seed.

JESUS COMPLETES HIS MISSION

As we reread the gospels now, we see that everything Jesus did while on earth was in fulfillment of the terms of the New Covenant agreement He had made with the Father. We see Him going after lost sheep, opening the eyes of the blind, raising the dead, flinging back the prison doors of death, speaking words of eternal life, doing good works, casting out devils and healing all manner of infirmities. In every verse of the gospels, Jesus fulfills the covenant. And He did none of these things on His own. Each one was what the Father had sent Him to do. Jesus was "keeping covenant" with the Father.

At the end of His life on earth, when Jesus prayed for His disciples at the Passover supper, we see once more the open-covenant dealings between Father and Son: "Now, O Father, glorify Me together with Yourself, with the glory which I had with You before the world was" (John 17:5). "Father, the hour has come. Glorify Your Son, that Your Son also may glorify You. . . . I have glorified You on the earth. I have finished the work which You have given Me to do" (John 17:1, 4).

With the cross before Him Jesus was about to fulfill all the covenant terms required of Him. And now, before He returned to glory, He brought before the Father the final terms of the covenant: "Father, You pledged in Our covenant to bring Me back to glory when I accomplished all You sent Me to do. Now I have fulfilled My part of the covenant—I have brought about the redemption of humankind, and I have made Your Body one.

Let's talk now about what's going to happen to My seed—all those who believe in Me."

Jesus was speaking as co-signer of the covenant. He said, "Now I am no longer in the world, but these are in the world, and I come to You. Holy Father, keep through Your name those whom You have given Me, that they may be one as We are" (John 17:11). He was saying to the Father, "We agreed that I could bring into our covenant everyone who trusts in Me. Now, Father, I ask You to bring these beloved ones under the same covenant promises You made to Me."

Jesus then said, "I do not pray that You should take them out of the world, but that You should keep them from the evil one. They are not of the world, just as I am not of the world" (John 17:15–16). Christ was saying, in essence, "You promised Me that You would be faithful to My seed. Now, Lord, sanctify them through Your truth. Make them holy and pure and keep them from the wicked one. Be with them in all their temptations. Let all the promises You gave Me be 'yea and amen' to them as well. Cause them to endure as You caused Me to endure."

The psalmist described this portion of the contract agreement like this:

> "He shall cry to Me, 'You are my Father, my God, and the rock of my salvation.' Also I will make him My firstborn, the highest of the kings of the earth. My mercy I will keep for him forever, and My covenant shall stand firm with him. His seed also I will make to endure forever, and his throne as the days of heaven.
>
> "If his sons forsake My law and do not walk in My judgments, if they break My statutes and do not keep My commandments, then I will punish their transgression with the rod, and their iniquity with stripes. Nevertheless My lovingkindness I will not utterly take from him, nor allow My faithfulness to fail. My covenant I will not break, nor alter the word that has gone out of My lips.

Once I have sworn by My holiness; I will not lie to David: His seed shall endure forever, and his throne as the sun before Me."

Psalm 89:26–36

The Son's sacrifice on the cross brought us into covenant agreement. Thus, this pledge of safety by the Father is made available to us as part of the covenant. The Father promised Jesus: "If You will go, I will keep and preserve every one of Your seed, just as I have kept and preserved You. I will never remove My faithfulness from You, nor from Your children. Your seed will endure to the end."

The covenant, cut before the world was formed, has in it the sworn oath of almighty God to save and deliver His people from the power and dominion of Satan. Faith in Christ brings us into God's covenant oath to keep us as faithfully as He kept His own Son.

WE ARE KEPT SAFE

So what does this covenant between Father and Son have to do with you and me? It is a picture of God's love for His beloved creation. He cut this covenant because He was unwilling to lose a single child to Satan. It is all about His undying love for His people.

The Father gave His Son, the Son gave His life, and we receive all the benefits. By mutual consent, the Father and Son made this covenant to keep and preserve the seed of Christ. It ensures that we will endure to the end.

THE EVIDENCE SPEAKS

The promise to save and deliver us, then, and our confidence that God will keep it, has a precedent in the relationship between Father and Son.

I could be free! I didn't have to resign myself to fighting the same battles day after day.

I was raised in a godly home and had a true and even passionate love for Jesus at a young age. As I got older I struggled through the rebellious attitude common among adolescents but never got mixed up in any kind of "bad sin." Despite not being in deep bondage, I still knew how it felt to be stuck. With all my heart I wanted to live for God and do what was right in His eyes, but almost daily I was frustrated by not being able to stop sinning.

As a result of my personal struggles, I eventually came to believe that fighting sin was what Christians do. We fight sin, hope we win, fail, repent, repeat. It was a sort of Darwinian Christianity where only the strong survive. Everything was about "resisting the devil" and "striving against sin." But none of it helped me overcome the exhaustion of continually fighting a battle I could never seem to win.

I first heard New Covenant teaching at Summit International School of Ministry (then Mount Zion). During those precious days as a student I heard a truth that filled me with hope and joy: I could be free! I did not have to resign myself to fighting the same battles day after day. The Christian can come to a place where his besetting sins are overcome by the power of the Holy Spirit, never to trouble him again. I was finally beginning to see that "He took captive those who had captured [me]" (Ephesians 4:8, GW), and that "having disarmed the powers and authorities, he made a public spectacle of them, triumphing over them by the cross" (Colossians 2:15, NIV).

I had it all backward! I had thought victory over sin was only for the strong, but I came to understand that my being a victorious Christian has nothing to do with the greatness of my efforts. It all rests on the greatness of the One who lives in me.

—*Nik*

Did the Father lead and guide Jesus, as He pledged He would? Did His Spirit empower the Son, giving Him encouragement and consolation? Did He bring Him through all of His temptations and trials? Did He keep Him from powers of darkness? Did He usher Him home to glory victorious? Was God true to His part of the covenant terms?

Yes, absolutely! And the Father who kept His covenant promises to His Son has pledged an eternal oath to do the same for us. Jesus affirmed this part of the covenant when He said,

> "The glory which You gave Me I have given them, that they may be one just as We are one: I in them, and You in Me; that they may be made perfect in one, and that the world may know that You have sent Me, and have loved them as You have loved Me."
>
> John 17:22–23

Christ secured us in the covenant made between the Father and Himself. In this prayer He was saying, "Father, look at Me and My seed as one person—I in them and they in Me. We are one person in covenant with You." Scripture promises that He "is able to keep [us] from stumbling, and to present [us] faultless before the presence of His glory with exceeding joy" (Jude 24).

God is not looking for people who have everything theologically straight. He wants those whose hearts are full of confidence in Him. By revealing to us His covenant with His Son, He wants to remove any doubts we may have about His ability to keep us. It is as if He is saying, "I'm going to make such a strong oath to you, you will have no other choice but to believe in Me."

We are to stay in Christ—abide in Him and trust Him. If we do this, we will surely see His glory. The words of promise are everlasting: "I have made a covenant with My chosen, I have sworn to My servant David: 'Your seed I will establish forever, and build up your throne to all generations'" (Psalm 89:3–4).

DISCUSSION
QUESTIONS

1. What is God talking about when He speaks of *covenant*? (Page 13)

2. What are common words still in use today that describe the meaning of covenant as it is used in Scripture? (Page 13)

3. What two key Scriptures in the book of Hebrews describe the eternal promises of the New Covenant? (Page 15)

4. Who is the "spiritual Israel" referred to in the apostle Paul's teaching? (Page 16)

5. For which Israel did God prepare the New Covenant? (Page 17)

6. In every covenant the agreement is between two primary parties. Who are the primary parties of the New Covenant? (Page 19)

7. What was God's principal purpose in making the New Covenant? (Page 19)

8. Read Isaiah 42:6. God made a covenant pledge to His Son. How is this pledge now made available to us? (Page 25)

2

FREEDOM FROM THE
DOMINION OF SIN

Now that we understand the foundation of the New Covenant into which we have entered with God, we can begin to appropriate its promises. One of the first steps we take is facing the truth that we cannot rescue ourselves from the power of sin. It is simply impossible for any believer to deliver himself from sin's dominion. That work can be accomplished only by the Holy Spirit.

This divine work is complicated by a twofold problem, however. God has to accomplish two things in us before He can deliver us from our besetting sins.

First, God has to inspire the sin-bound person to want to be free. By nature, man does not want to be delivered from his sin. He simply will not respond to a gracious mercy call. So, God has to implement a plan or device that will allow a person to see the exceeding wickedness of his sin. This person has to become sin-sick, aware of how wicked and devastating his sin is, before he will yearn for deliverance. He has to come to his wits' end, where he sees he is being ruined by sin—helpless, wretched, empty, ensnared and deceived by sin, and laden down with guilt.

Second, God has to cause the sin-bound person to see the utter futility of his own efforts to set himself free. Man remains convinced he can cut off his own chains. He thinks if he struggles hard enough or works out the correct formula, he will be able to free himself from Satan's grip. The Lord, therefore, has to bring him to a point of total surrender, where he submits his struggle completely into God's hands.

How does the Lord accomplish these two things? How does He cause the sin-bound person, first, to see his transgressions as exceedingly sinful, and, second, to give up the fight in his flesh, admitting, "I can't do it. I'm helpless to free myself from this sin. Lord, You have to do it in me"?

Scripture explains that this twofold work is accomplished in us by the Old Covenant. Indeed, we cannot fully understand or appropriate the blessing of the New Covenant until the Old Covenant has accomplished this dual work in us.

By its very design, the Old Covenant of works was intended to teach enslaved man how high and holy his heavenly Father is. The Ten Commandments, for example, give us a picture of what is known as the moral law. This is a representation of the heart and nature of God—a nature of holiness, purity, righteousness. It sets a standard so high no human can possibly reach it in his own strength.

After giving man these commandments, God then commanded him to obey His Law perfectly. In fact, anyone who failed to keep a single law was guilty of violating them all. That person might love God, be a faithful spouse and do good works, but if he had even the slightest adulterous or idolatrous thought in his heart, he would be breaking the entire covenant. God said, "Now therefore, if you will indeed obey My voice and keep My covenant, then you shall be a . . . holy nation" (Exodus 19:5–6). "Obey My voice, and I will be your God, and you shall be My people" (Jeremiah 7:23).

You may wonder, "Why would God make a covenant He knew no one could keep?" Simply put, it was the only way God could bring man to the end of himself—to cause him to see the futility of relying on his own strength to be holy. This is why Paul called the Old Covenant "the ministry of death" (2 Corinthians 3:7). He knew it requires of us a kind of dying. In plain language, we all must die to any attempt to establish our own righteousness, and to any thought that we can deliver ourselves from sin's strongholds.

The moral law is also meant to make man see his guilt: "By the law is the knowledge of sin . . . that every mouth may be stopped, and all the world may become guilty before God" (Romans 3:20, 19). Once we see our iniquity soberly, we are silenced by its exceeding sinfulness. "Moreover the law entered that the offense might abound" (Romans 5:20). Through the revelation of the Law, our sins become offensive to us—disturbing, sickening, overwhelming.

By setting His standard of holiness so high, God was proving to man that he could never attain the Law in his own strength. Instead, He was placing man in a school—a place where he would be taught how utterly wicked and sinful he was. By graduation time, he should be a dead man—dead to any hope he might have of freeing himself from the bondage of sin.

Likewise today, as long as we have the slightest idea we can achieve holiness on our own, we are still living under the Old Covenant's ministration of death. God's whole idea behind implementing this covenant is to send us to our death.

After studying this aspect of the covenant, I wrote the following conclusion in my journal:

> The Old Covenant has finished its work. It has put me on my face—empty, helpless, wounded, weak—and now it can fade away. I am fully persuaded that I cannot by human strength and will obey or please God. I have no plea of holiness. I am without strength, and I can do nothing in my own ability. My sin is too powerful, the chains too heavy. I am too wicked to free myself. I need a miracle, and I need a helper. All I can do now is cry, Abba, Father.

WHICH COVENANT DEFINES YOUR WALK?

Let me tell you how you can know if the Old Covenant has finished its work in you, and whether or not you are ready to move into the glory of the New Covenant.

Think about this question: What is your reaction whenever you slip and fall, returning to your old habit or lust once more? Do you go to your prayer closet, fall on your face and begin wailing, "Oh, Father, I promise not to do it anymore"? Do you shout at God, asking, "Lord, where were You when I needed You? Why didn't You give me the power to resist this temptation? Where was the Holy Spirit to stop me from giving in?" Do you wallow in self-examination, trying to find some new measure of commitment to recover and move on?

If either one of the above scenarios describes your reaction to failure or sin, you are still living under the Old Covenant. Your cry probably comes directly from your flesh, not from God's Spirit in you. Your flesh feels sorry for itself because it did not accomplish the deliverance. And now it is asking for one more opportunity, begging, "Hang in there with me—try me one more time."

Grasping the truth of the New Covenant saved my marriage.

The first time I read Pastor David Wilkerson's teaching on the New Covenant, I cried. I read it again and cried some more. Then the third time I read it, I shouted, "I'm free!" On the next reading, I highlighted passages and shared it with others.

The freedom that came from grasping the truth of the New Covenant and what Jesus did for me saved my walk with Him and saved my marriage. I have worn out three copies of the book. I refer to it constantly in discussions with friends and I have lost count of the number of books I have sent to others.

I was born again as a college student, fell in love with Jesus and followed Him to the best of my ability. Then the struggles of life and the challenges of raising a family, making ends meet and building a career overshadowed my personal commitment to the Lord. My own strength was gone and I was powerless to overcome sin.

Interestingly enough, in reading about the New Covenant, I realized that it was more about His commitment to me than about my trying to serve Him. The very thought of this truth scrambled the brains of my doctrine about serving God.

The pillars of the New Covenant have changed my life as I realize:

> His love is greater than my sin, and He has the power to break sin's dominion.

> At the cross, all self-dependency was demolished. My efforts are ineffective, and I leave them at the cross.

> He is my High Priest and my Intercessor. He alone stands for me.

It is so liberating to walk under His authority as my Lord and my provider. I believe I am a better husband and father as a result. I am also more effective in representing who Christ is since I am not under the weight of self-dependency.

—Jerry

This is an ongoing problem with many Christians. We look to the Holy Spirit as some kind of booster shot to empower or energize our human will. We expect Him to build up our supply of grit and determination, so we can stand up to temptation the next time it comes. We cry, "Make me strong, Lord! Give me an iron will, so I can withstand all sin." But God knows this would only make our flesh stronger, enabling it to boast.

I want you to examine yourself: What has all your crying, grieving and questioning brought you? Do you now enjoy lasting freedom or do you occasionally go back to your sin? Are your times of repentance increasingly marked by more tears, louder crying and deeper despair—with no sign of deliverance from bondage?

If the Old Covenant had truly done its work in you, you would already be "dead." You would not have any tears left, any strength to cry out, any confidence in your flesh whatsoever. The truth is, most of our weeping, begging and striving comes from our continuing expectation that something good can rise up out of our human nature to offer the Lord. But that simply is never going to happen. We are always going to be too weak and frail in our flesh to produce holiness. Yes, we are commanded to be strong—but only in the power of God's might, and not our own.

Please do not misunderstand me. I emphatically believe there is such a thing as godly sorrow over sin. Such sorrow produces true repentance. And I believe there are acceptable tears that flow from the hearts of those who grieve over wounding Christ. If you have never prayed from this place of repentance, you might want to do so now.

Lord, I confess my inability to obey Your commandments. I acknowledge my utter helplessness to deliver myself from sin's dominion. In all my strivings to get free, I have failed again and again. So now I come to You as "dead"—in full surrender. I confess my need to be delivered from my sin—and I admit I cannot do it on my own.

Oh, Lord, Your Old Covenant has accomplished in me two important things. First, I know in my heart that I want to be free. I truly want You to crush sin's dominion over me. I don't want to excuse my sin anymore, and I don't want to be given over to it. My heart's desire is to be holy and blameless before You. Whatever it takes, Father, I want to be delivered. I want to live wholly dependent on Your power.

Second, I have abandoned all hope of ever getting free by my own strength. I realize my only hope of freedom from slavery rests in Your power. I come to You now by faith, Lord, casting myself into Your hands. Show me the blessings and provisions of Your New Covenant. I need a new revelation, a new arrangement. The old one has only brought me to despair.

Thank You, Lord. In Jesus' name I pray, Amen.

UNDERSTANDING THIS NEW AGREEMENT

If you have prayed that prayer from your heart, then the blessing of the New Covenant is yours. I remind you now of God's pronouncement of this covenant, as described by the author of Hebrews:

> "Behold, the days are coming, says the LORD, when I will make a new covenant with the house of Israel and with the house of Judah—not according to the covenant that I made with their fathers in the day when I took them by the hand to lead them out of the land of Egypt."
>
> Hebrews 8:8–9

God said to His people, "I am going to make a new agreement with you. It will not be like the old one that I made with your

35

fathers. This covenant will be better, because it will be based on better promises."

Embedded in this New Covenant is a great and glorious blessing, which is outlined in the book of Acts:

> "You are sons of the prophets, and of the covenant which God made with our fathers, saying to Abraham, 'And in your seed all the families of the earth shall be blessed.' To you first, God, having raised up His Servant Jesus, sent Him to bless you, in turning away every one of you from your iniquities."
>
> Acts 3:25–26

God spoke this message to a people who had failed Him utterly. He was assuring them, "I have invested all power, authority and riches in My Son. And now I have raised Him up to bless you."

What wonderful news for the sin-bound Christian today! He has been burdened down and defeated by the power of sin, so he comes into God's presence cowering, feeling guilty, condemned and helpless. He wonders, "How could the Lord bless me? I have sinned against the light of His Word. I've failed Him." Whenever he prays, he waits for sin's curse to fall on him, looking for judgment to strike. But now he is given these incredible words: "I have sent My Son to bless you, by turning you away from your sins."

God did not send His Son to take vengeance on hungering, thirsting seekers. Jesus came to save! That was the whole reason He went to the cross. "For God did not send His Son into the world to condemn the world, but that the world through Him might be saved" (John 3:17).

Christ is the seed of blessing God promised to give Abraham. Look again at Acts 3:25–26: "In your seed all the families of the earth shall be blessed." And God the Father sent this seed

to fulfill His covenant promise of blessing. The glorious blessing is that we can be "turned away" from our iniquities. "God,
having raised up His Servant Jesus, sent Him to bless you, in
turning away every one of you from your iniquities." The Lord
says, "The greatest way I can bless you is to deliver you from
your sin—to break its power and dominion over you."

Many of the ancient Jews expected a different kind of blessing through this covenant promise. They had their own concept
of blessing. They were convinced the Messiah would come to
earth to set up an opulent society for them, showering them with
wealth, prosperity and unending happiness. They thought He
would give them all of the world's resources and positions of
power so that they would not have to labor or strive anymore.
Even today, some Christians expect this kind of kingdom to be
manifested on earth.

But God says, "The greatest blessing I can give to sin-bound
souls is to free them from sin's grip through the blessing of My
Son's ministry." An angel of the Lord told Joseph in a dream
that his betrothed, Mary, would bear a son. "And you shall call
His name JESUS, for He will save His people from their sins"
(Matthew 1:21).

Today, every heaven-hungry believer who is bound by sin
knows the value of this incredible blessing. Take, for example, a
minister friend of mine. This man enjoyed fifteen years of freedom from a serious drug addiction. He even served as director
of a successful drug rehabilitation program. Then one day he
fell back into his old heroin habit—and sin's dominion came
over his life once again.

After each fix, this minister's spirit was crushed. He would go
into his office, shut the door, lie prostrate on the floor and weep
and sob loudly, begging God to deliver him. He cried, "How
could I have done this to You, Lord? What kind of man am I

to have betrayed Your great kindness to me? Oh, how wicked I must be!" His repentance was so dramatic that his face grew red and raw from rubbing against the carpet in anguish.

I believe that if you had offered this tormented man a choice between a fortune that would last a lifetime, or freedom from his drug habit, he would have reached for the blessing of deliverance. Being set free from the dominion of sin and its guilt is the greatest blessing he could have received.

The Lord has made just such provision for us, offering us deliverance. Moreover, His New Covenant promise does even more than provide pardon and forgiveness. Scripture says the Spirit of God actually "subdues" our sins and turns us from them: "He will again have compassion on us, and will subdue our iniquities. You will cast all our sins into the depths of the sea" (Micah 7:19). Think of it! Not I, but my God, will subdue and conquer all my sins, by the inner working of the Holy Spirit.

How God Turns Us from Sin

If you believe God's Word about forgiving and pardoning our sins, but have difficulty believing His promise to subdue our sins and turn us from our iniquities, then you are not alone. Many people struggle with this concept. Yet, under the New Covenant, the battle is not ours; it is the work of God's Spirit. Indeed, Jesus has invested all of His might and power in the Holy Spirit for this battle.

The Holy Spirit is the great gift of the New Covenant, and He was sent to do in us what we cannot do in our own ability or strength. He is the one, after all, who wooed each of us to Christ, and now He has been given all power and authority to thwart sin's dominion over our lives. In fact, if we do not have

God's Spirit dwelling in us, then we do not belong to Christ. The Holy Spirit does nothing isolated from the cross and the implanted grace of Christ.

I ask you: If you throw yourself on the mercy of the Holy Spirit—trusting Him completely, believing He is able to fulfill everything God demands of you—what enemy could stand against His power to accomplish all things in you? What temptation could overwhelm His might, which abides in you? The Holy Spirit simply asks that we come to Him believing that He has all power and authority to break sin's dominion over us.

Please understand that this New Covenant promise does not apply to Christians who are not convicted or troubled by their sins. It offers nothing to believers whose theology allows them to continue in their iniquities. Such people are libertines, turning the grace of God into lasciviousness. But to every lover of Jesus who hates his or her sin—those whose one great desire is to walk righteously before the Lord—the New Covenant offers power from above to destroy sin's dominion.

Make no mistake—God expects perfect obedience under the New Covenant just as He did under the Old. Thus, Paul urges us, "If by the Spirit you put to death the deeds of the body, you will live" (Romans 8:13). Our Lord has never once winked at our sin, nor has He eased up on His call to holiness.

Now, however, He has given us His very own Spirit to fulfill in us all of the Law's demands. This does not mean we are suddenly able to achieve sinless perfection. Nor does it mean that the Spirit will do this work without our cooperation. Rather, it means that just as Christ's sacrifice and perfect obedience suffice for us, so His Spirit subdues our sins and crushes their dominion over us, through our faith in the New Covenant promises.

How does the Holy Spirit do this in us? How does He break the power of sinful bondage in our lives? I honestly do not

Walking in New Covenant truth is knowing that my battles are not really mine—they are God's.

I came to Jesus out of a homosexual background. Through the years I often questioned why God allowed same-sex attraction in my life. Did He make a mistake when He made me? Am I a black sheep, a "devil child"? Maybe God just forgot about me somewhere along the line. Even after accepting Jesus as my Savior, I still asked these questions.

I realized that my path to freedom is something I am totally unable to accomplish in my own strength. On my own, I am too weak to withstand temptation and do what I know is right.

Even though my emotions fluctuate and my personal life goes up and down, God's standard of truth does not change. The path to freedom is His work, not something I can do through my own efforts. And it certainly is not something that happens because of what I deserve.

Walking in His New Covenant truth is not a magical, easy journey. It is simply knowing that my battles are not really mine—they are God's. He will fight these battles—and will win—and He will help me if I ask Him. Understanding the New Covenant teachings and walking in His love, mercy, grace and power is the only path of lasting victory for me.

—Jack

know. His ways are past finding out. But one thing is crystal clear: Our part is simply to trust that He will do everything Christ sent Him to do.

We are also to be encouraged by the evidence we see of His divine work in us. He convicts us, opens God's Word to us, anoints our eyes and ears to see and hear His eternal truth and takes possession of our hearts as we respond to His wooing. He lovingly warns us and chastens us. He sometimes removes temptations from our hearts and oftentimes He makes Christ so real to us, it drives from our hearts all desire to sin.

God has sworn by an oath to give us a new heart—one that is inclined to obey: "I will give them a heart to know Me, that I am the LORD; and they shall be My people, and I will be their God, for they shall return to Me with their whole heart" (Jeremiah 24:7). Also, He states: "I will give you a new heart and put a new spirit within you; I will take the heart of stone out of your flesh and give you a heart of flesh" (Ezekiel 36:26).

God fulfills His covenant with us not only to give us a new heart, but also to write His commands on our hearts. In other words, He promises to cause us to know Him. Again, the Holy Spirit is the one who accomplishes this work in us. He teaches us about the Father's nature and ways—and, in the process, He transforms us into Christ's divine image.

Our Lord has sworn a sovereign oath to be merciful to us in our struggles against sin. And until full victory comes, He will be patient and loving with us, never casting us aside. He promises, "No matter what I demand of you, I will supply you with all the power you need to accomplish it. I won't ask anything of you for which I have not made provision."

The same power that raised Jesus from the dead—and which enabled Him to fulfill God's Law through a perfect, sinless life—now abides in us. God's own Spirit is alive in us, providing all power over every work the enemy tries to bring against us. He promises to demolish all demonic strongholds.

But you may ask, "What about our part?" Our part is not easy. Faith never is. Yet that is the requirement in submitting to the Holy Spirit's work. By faith, we are to cast ourselves completely into His care and trust Him to lead us out of every satanic snare: "'Not by might nor by power, but by My Spirit,' says the LORD of hosts" (Zechariah 4:6).

When the enemy comes flooding into your soul, enticing you toward an old lust, call upon the Holy Spirit. Listen to His every whisper and obey His every command. Do not shut Him out. His deliverance will not work for you if you do not really want to hear what He has to say. But if you are prepared to do whatever He empowers you to do, He will not withhold His word from you. You will hear Him behind you, saying, "This is the way—walk in it."

You can move out of the Old Covenant and into the New in a single step. It happens when you see how impossible it is for you to overcome sin by your own human efforts. It dawns on you that a covenant-making God has sworn to give the Holy Spirit to all believers who ask and that He will accomplish in you what the Lord has promised by oath. So, finally, you abandon yourself totally to God and His promises. You believe He will perform what He has promised.

DISCUSSION QUESTIONS

1. God wants us to be free from the dominion of sin for two reasons. What are those reasons? (Pages 29–30)

2. What does the Old Covenant of works teach us? (Page 30)

3. What is your reaction when you slip and fall back into sin? (Page 32)

4. The Old Covenant accomplishes what two important things in us? (Pages 29–30)

5. Read Acts 3:25–26. Within the New Covenant is a great blessing. (Page 36) Read Matthew 1:21. Why is this important? (Page 37)

6. Read Micah 7:19. The New Covenant promise does more than provide pardon and forgiveness. Scripture says the Holy Spirit will do what with our sins? (Page 38)

7. What is the great gift of the New Covenant? (Page 38)

8. What should be our response to the work of the Holy Spirit in us? (Pages 39, 41)

9. Read Jeremiah 24:7 and Ezekiel 36:26. God is making a covenant with us to do what two things? (Page 41)

10. What is our requirement when faced with the traps of the enemy? (Page 42)

3

THE CROSS AND THE
NEW COVENANT

It is the basis of Christian doctrine that only the cross of Jesus
Christ can make us acceptable to God. No works of the flesh,
no human goodness—however meritorious—can ever contribute
to a person's salvation. The cross annihilated the concept of
works as righteousness.

This point of doctrine is the reason why the cross was such
an offense, or stumbling block, to the Jews of Jesus' day. First-
century Jews were steeped in legalism. They were trained from
childhood to believe they could earn eternal salvation by strict
adherence to the Law of Moses, including the ceremonial ordinances with more than six hundred rules and regulations. One
of the unyielding requirements of the Mosaic Law was male
circumcision, the cutting of the flesh.

The first church in Jerusalem held on to this legalism. That
body, which came together after Peter's sermon at Pentecost, was

made up mostly of Jewish believers. Many of those Jews were priests who had given their lives to observance of the Law. And now, even after their conversion, they preached a mixture of faith in Christ and the keeping of the Law, including circumcision. Scripture says they taught that "unless you are circumcised according to the custom of Moses, you cannot be saved" (Acts 15:1).

These men, in essence, claimed this: "Yes, Jesus died for our sins. But our faith in His work on the cross does not provide us with complete salvation. We still have to observe the Law—to do our best to contribute to our salvation by keeping the rules and ordinances Moses gave us. Submitting to the rite of circumcision is part of that."

This incensed the apostle Paul. He saw it as a deadly mixture and spoke against it boldly. He told the leaders at Jerusalem, "Your rules and ordinances are no longer of any value whatsoever. The cross of Christ has abolished them all."

This point of doctrine appears in many of Paul's letters to the early churches. He wrote: "[Jesus] abolished in His flesh the enmity, that is, the law of commandments contained in ordinances, so as to create in Himself one new man from the two, thus making peace" (Ephesians 2:15).

> Therefore, if you died with Christ from the basic principles of the world, why, as though living in the world, do you subject yourselves to regulations—"Do not touch, do not taste, do not handle," which all concern things which perish with the using—according to the commandments and doctrines of men?
>
> Colossians 2:20–22

He also wrote that Jesus "wiped out the handwriting of requirements that was against us, which was contrary to us. And He has taken it out of the way, having nailed it to the cross" (verse 14).

As we read these passages today, we see that it was impossible for any Jewish convert to overlook Paul's meaning. He was telling them plainly, "Anything that you think secures your salvation other than the blood of Jesus Christ is worthless. All your works of flesh intended to make you righteous before God are empty, void, finished. Jesus drove a nail through them all."

You can imagine how offensive Paul's words were to these striving, burdened-down Jewish believers. All their lives, they had gone about the dreary work of struggling with the Law, trying to earn God's favor. They had diligently observed the ceremonial washing of hands and eating utensils. They had traveled only lawfully prescribed distances on the Sabbath. They had made sure they never touched or shook hands with a Gentile, or even allowed their clothes to swish against them. They repeated long, tedious prayers, chanted for hours at a time and studied the Law under scribes and Pharisees. Every night they took a spiritual inventory of their deeds, and were downcast when they discovered they had failed to observe a jot or tittle of the Law. They lived under immense guilt and condemnation, because their consciences kept accusing them of failure.

These people had spent lifetimes trying to earn their salvation, and now Paul was telling them that all those years of works were worthless. Can you hear those priests objecting to Paul? "How dare you say this to us? Do you actually expect us to disown our years of struggle, pain and striving? Are we suddenly no longer to trust in the act of circumcision, after years of believing that this mark on our flesh seals our acceptance before God? How can this ancient rite that Moses gave us suddenly be worthless? Everything you're telling us is an offense to us."

Yet that is the offense of the cross. It says: "You have no power or means to gain favor with God, other than coming to the finished work of Jesus in repentance and faith. There is no goodness in your flesh whatsoever—nothing you can offer the Lord on your own. Any righteousness you may think you have achieved is filthy rags in His sight, according to His Word."

Some of the Jews tried to muddy the waters by spreading rumors that Paul agreed with their mixed doctrine, but he was quick to set the record straight. He wrote: "And I, brethren, if I still preach circumcision, why do I still suffer persecution? Then the offense of the cross has ceased" (Galatians 5:11).

Paul was saying, "Wait just a minute! You all know I preach faith in Christ as the only way to salvation, and everybody knows that's an offense to you. It offends you that the cross did away with all your striving in the flesh, all your legalistic rules and regulations. That offense is the very reason you are persecuting me.

"If I preached your gospel of mixture, you would accept me. You would even applaud me, because I would have removed the part of my message that is so offensive to you. But if that is the case, then why am I still being persecuted at your hands? If I have compromised my stand against your dead works of the flesh, then why do you still fight me so? Why does the circumcision crowd still hold such animosity toward me? You know my message well, brothers. Our salvation is not by works, but by faith in Christ alone."

THE MODERN BENT TOWARD LEGALISM

Multitudes of Christians today, including many ministers, still have not died to their own legalistic attitudes. Indeed, in every major city in America and all around the world, different denominations hold various standards for the Gospel. These mandate certain terms of acceptance before God—all kinds of manmade rules. Yet these modern standards come from the same deadly, man-centered attitudes that Paul warned the Colossians about: "Don't touch that, don't eat this, don't wear improper makeup or dress," and on and on.

Of course I believe in high standards for Christians, including decent dress codes, holy living and separation from the world. But God help us if we even hint to people that any such observance can ever make us acceptable in His eyes.

Many believers remain under constant bondage to some doctrine of works because they think it makes them holy. They simply do not want to believe that all their sacrifices through the years are for naught. And so, when they hear the message of the cross—that no human striving or works can save us, and that only the grace of Christ assures our salvation—they become offended. They cry out, as the first-century Jewish converts did, "You're teaching permissiveness. You don't believe in holiness anymore."

Nothing could be further from the truth. Only one person is holy—Jesus Christ—and all our holiness must come through faith in Him. Let me show you how profound the words and acts of Jesus are on this subject.

THE DISCIPLES' MISSTEP

Matthew 18 begins with an amazing scene. Peter, James and John had just accompanied Jesus down from the Mount of Transfiguration, where they had experienced the Lord's awesome presence. Yet, inexplicably, the disciples suddenly began arguing about who among them would be the greatest in the Kingdom of heaven.

These men should have been humbled by their incredible experience. It should have revealed to them the sinfulness of human nature in the light of God's pure holiness. Instead, the Twelve began trying to measure their relationship to Jesus by all the good works they had done. They started tallying up how much they had sacrificed for Him, each claiming, "I've done much more to please our Master than the rest of you. I've been more devoted, more faithful, more giving."

We cannot know, of course, all the things the disciples said in this scene, but Scripture does give insight into their nature. I can readily imagine the words of impetuous, hot-headed Peter. He might have said: "Gentlemen, I can settle this argument right now. Think about it—I just came down from the mountain of glory. I saw things there I'm not even allowed to talk to you about. God actually spoke to me! And may I remind you who it was who walked on water with our Lord? If anyone has earned a place near Jesus' throne, it's yours truly."

The others were not far behind in their self-assessments. These blinded men had missed it altogether. Here we see a picture of Old Covenant competition—the kind of willful striving that leads to an attitude of superiority. The truth is, it does not matter what kind of great revelations you have received, or how boldly you witness, or how powerfully you preach, or how many demons you may have cast out of people. Not one of those things counts with God. If you trust in any of them over Christ's finished work for your acceptance in God's eyes, you are stating that His death on the cross was of no effect.

As we read Matthew 18, we have to remember that in everything Jesus did during His ministry on earth, He was laying a foundation for His future Church. We know from Revelation that the twelve disciples were the foundation stones of His Church, the formative material Christ used to build His edifice. And now, as the Lord listened to His disciples arguing, He must have been absolutely appalled.

WHAT JESUS DID

All through the New Testament, God's people are referred to as children—children of God, children of the Kingdom, children of the bride chamber, children of the promise. When Paul addressed the believers in Galatia as "my little children," he was referring to baby converts, those in whom Christ is being formed.

Now, as Jesus overheard His disciples, He had to be concerned for all the "babes" who would be brought into His Church to sit under their ministry—multitudes of immature, untaught, innocent converts.

Soon, during the Passover with His disciples, He would be holding the cup of the New Covenant. His death would signal the end of the Old Covenant of works. The efforts of human flesh to gain acceptance by God would no longer be viable. All merit before God would have to come through faith in Him alone. He could not allow His Church to be built on a doctrinal mixture of the Law and the cross—otherwise, the new converts in their care would think, "I can earn my salvation," and try to work their way into God's graces.

So, what did Jesus do? Matthew tells us Christ called a little child to Him and took the youngster in His arms. He wanted to give His disciples a profound illustrated sermon. He told them:

> "Assuredly, I say to you, unless you are converted and become as little children, you will by no means enter the kingdom of heaven. Therefore whoever humbles himself as this little child is the greatest in the kingdom of heaven. Whoever receives one little child like this in My name receives Me."
>
> Matthew 18:3–5

In these three verses, Jesus laid out the kind of relationship He desires with His people. He was saying, "Look at this child.

Here is My future Church. This young one represents every new believer who is going to come to Me in childlike faith, from every nation, race and tribe. I tell you, My Church must relate to Me as this child does."

Make no mistake—Jesus was issuing a strong rebuke to His disciples here. When He said to them, "Unless you are converted," they had to wonder, "Us, be converted? We're His chosen disciples. What's the Master talking about?"

The Greek word Jesus used for *converted* means "a sharp twist." Christ was telling these men: "You must undergo a sudden turning, a sharp twist, in your theology. You have to turn away quickly from all your thoughts of how to become special in My Kingdom through your own works. That is the Old Covenant—and it is about to pass away."

Jesus wanted to strike a deathblow to this deadly doctrinal mixture once and for all. So, next He called for His disciples to humble themselves completely. He commanded them, "Become as little children." He was telling them, "I'm building My Church on you, and if you want any part in it, you must become as humble as this little child I am holding in My arms."

According to some Christian scholars, Jesus was trying to teach us in this passage that we need to adopt childlike attitudes and behavior in order to be godly. I do not see that in His words here. Rather, I believe He is asking us for two simple things: repudiation of all self-dependency, and uncomplicated devotion. These traits, Jesus said, will characterize us as true Kingdom servants: "Whoever humbles himself as this little child is the greatest in the Kingdom of heaven. Whoever receives one little child like this in My name receives Me."

Oh, what complicated theology and doctrines we have invented! Yet the Lord foresaw all of this. He knew denominations would arise with stipulations to faith, such as, "You must observe

This greater understanding of the New Covenant began to unlock the Scriptures, and it is my firm belief that this teaching brings you back to your first love.

In the beginning of 1998, David Wilkerson began a series of in-depth teachings on the New Covenant at Times Square Church. I thought I understood the topic, having my degree in theology; however, the real revelation of it had not registered with me. In fact, it took a year and many messages on the topic before I received the illumination from the Holy Spirit.

I remember well the day the understanding came. It was November 1998, and the title of the sermon Brother Dave preached was "Beware of Dogs." During the preaching of this message, the revelation of the completed New Covenant—which was made between the Father and the Son and excludes any effort on our part—hit me like a thunderbolt. Overwhelming joy filled my heart and both relief and release from a "works" gospel were made manifest.

I remember the subsequent walks with my wife in Central Park, where we talked nonstop about how this incredible truth had escaped our knowledge for so long, but how thrilled we were to be walking in it. This greater understanding of the New Covenant began to unlock all the Scriptures in a new dimension. In fact, it is my firm belief that this teaching brings you back to your first love. You see, the New Covenant returns you to understanding that it is God's love toward you and not you trying to recapture your love toward Him.

Brother Dave told me repeatedly, "You cannot have an ongoing revival without the knowledge of the New Covenant." If the only reason I was a part of Times Square Church for twelve years was to gain this understanding, then I owe my life and ministry today to Brother Dave and this message. I know this teaching of the New Covenant has had equal impact on many, but I consider my life to have been the most changed.

—*Neil*

the standards of our group." "You must venerate Jesus' mother, Mary." "You must be baptized in our church to be saved."

While the scribes and Pharisees argued about Jesus' birthplace, the circumstances of His childhood, where and when He might have gained His spiritual knowledge—the children of Christ's day simply came running when He called them. They flung themselves into His loving arms, with no questions, doubts or arguments. They did not have to figure Him out; they just loved Him.

We see the children's devotion to Him described in Matthew 21. In this passage, the Temple visitors and moneychangers were busily involved in their religious activities and legalistic functions, trying to gain favor with God. But consider what the children were doing: "The children [were] crying out in the temple and saying, 'Hosanna to the Son of David!'" (Matthew 21:15). Those young ones were busy worshiping Jesus.

Please do not misunderstand me—I believe doctrine is essential. We need to understand important theological concepts such as justification by faith and sanctification. But if our knowledge of these things does not produce life in us, it is all just dead-letter.

On the other hand, those who come to Jesus in childlike devotion receive true spiritual understanding. "If anyone wills to do His will, he shall know concerning the doctrine, whether it is from God or whether I speak on My own authority" (John 7:17). Christ is saying here, "Simply love Me as these trusting children do. Then you will gain understanding. I have brought a New Covenant to you, and I have done away with all the rules and regulations. All I ask is that you run into My arms and trust Me to give you everything you need. I will teach you about the obedience of love."

Many pastors, especially, need to be converted from their "I can do it" theology. Their thinking needs to take a sharp turn from the foolish spirit of competition—works of flesh that focus on who has the biggest church building, the biggest congregation, the biggest budget, the best music, the best praise meetings. They need to turn from their constant search for new ways to get results. And they need to get back to the secret closet of prayer—to dependence on God rather than on man.

A WORD OF WARNING

Jesus issued a severe warning to any who teach that the cross is not sufficient to save the lost:

> "Whoever causes one of these little ones who believe in Me to sin, it would be better for him if a millstone were hung around his neck, and he were drowned in the depth of the sea. Woe to the world because of offenses! For offenses must come, but woe to that man by whom the offense comes!"
>
> Matthew 18:6–7

Jesus was expressing His wrath toward those who teach that the cross is not sufficient to save. Note that He was not speaking to hardened Pharisees or doubting Jews. No, He was talking to the very foundation stones of His Church: His own disciples. He was warning them not to be offended by the New Covenant. They had to accept the truth that He alone is full payment for our sins.

Likewise, Jesus is telling the Church today: "Woe to any preacher, teacher or witness who puts a stumbling block before any of these baby converts. They come to Me in simple faith and repentance, and you will incur My wrath if you offend them by saying, 'Jesus is not enough. If you really want to be saved, you must do more. Here are the specific doctrines and rules of our church.'"

Does this happen in your church? What if a young woman comes into your congregation wearing black lipstick, skintight clothes and a spiked purple hairdo? Maybe she is sick and tired of her life, and all she wants is to know Christ. She has been praying, "Jesus, if You are real, please show Yourself to me."

Yet along comes someone who is horrified at her appearance and says, "I'm sorry, miss, you can't be a Christian and look that way. You have to get rid of that black lipstick. And make sure you don't ever come to church wearing those tight pants again. Shame on you."

Or, maybe a young man with long hair and the smell of alcohol walks into your worship service. He has just been saved off the street and is seeking the reality of Christ in a church fellowship.

Yet someone in your congregation walks up to him and says, "Young man, you've got to cut your hair. And what's that smell on you—beer? I'm not sure if you're really saved. If you want to serve God, you've got to change. You can't be a Christian and look or smell that way."

Of course I believe that drunkenness is evil, and that women should dress modestly. But young believers need to be allowed time for the Holy Spirit to deal with them about these issues. Every babe in Christ needs the Church's full love and support until he or she can be shown the right way.

Pastors, evangelists, teachers—let the seriousness of Jesus' harsh words in Matthew 18 sink into your soul: "It would be better for him if a millstone were hung around his neck, and he were drowned in the depth of the sea." Seldom in all the Bible does God speak so harshly on a subject as Jesus does here.

Nothing aroused the wrath of Jesus more than an attack on His truth. We think we see His wrath at full peak when He drove the moneychangers out of the Temple, but that is nothing as compared to the indictment He brought here. His words were strong because any mixture of works and the cross could bring down the entire Church.

I know a Russian pastor who preaches that no one's salvation is complete until he or she has suffered. This man once told me, "Your congregation has no right to rejoice until you've all paid your dues with hard times."

No—never! As a minister of God, I tremble as I hear what Jesus is telling His Church here: If any of us, in any form of ministry, advocates man-made moral codes, legalistic rules or any other human standards as being necessary to salvation, we face the holy wrath of God Himself. If we burden down any child of Jesus with our own denominational standards, we would be better off drowned at sea.

A PERPLEXING SCRIPTURE

Now we come to one of the most misunderstood passages in all of Scripture—what is known as the "mutilation passage." Jesus told His disciples this:

> "Wherefore if thy hand or thy foot offend thee [causes you to sin, NKJV], cut them off, and cast them from thee: it is better . . . to enter into life halt or maimed, rather than having two hands or two feet to be cast into everlasting fire. And if thine eye offend thee, pluck it out, and cast it from thee: it is better . . . to enter into life with one eye, rather than having two eyes to be cast into hell fire."
>
> Matthew 18:8–9, KJV

Jesus began this passage with the word *wherefore*, meaning, "in light of this." He was tying His statement here into the context of the lesson He had been teaching about mixing works with the cross. So, when He said here, "If your hand or foot or eye offend you," He was talking about the offense that the cross brings to the flesh.

We find further clarification in the letter of the apostle Paul to the Galatians, for he took up this same teaching. Remember that the Jewish believers in that church were entangling the children of Christ with a yoke of bondage, insisting that all believers must be circumcised in order to be saved. As we noted, Paul rebuked all who taught this in no uncertain terms. Here are his words to the Galatians:

> You have become estranged from Christ, you who attempt to be justified by law; you have fallen from grace. For we through the Spirit eagerly wait for the hope of righteousness by faith. For in Christ Jesus neither circumcision nor uncircumcision avails anything, but faith working through love.
>
> Galatians 5:4–6

Do you hear what he is saying? Paul told the Galatians that by choosing works over the cross they had fallen from grace. Now listen to what the apostle added: "I could wish that those who trouble you would even cut themselves off!" (verse 12). The original Greek implies something significant. Paul was saying, "I would to God your works-oriented teachers would mutilate themselves."

Everyone hearing this letter knew what Paul meant. A principal city of Galatia called Pessinus was known for its worship of a goddess named Cybele. Her devoted followers were called Apocopi, and their sacrifices included self-mutilation—beating their own backs until they were bloody.

Paul was telling the Galatians, "If you're going to try to bypass the cross by trusting in the cutting of your flesh to please God, then why not go all the way? Join the flagellants, the Apocopi, and literally mutilate your bodies. After all, if your theology is right, then a little bit of cutting is not enough; a lot is holier. Do as the Apocopi do."

If you do not stand on the foundation of the finished work of Jesus at the cross, then where does the cutting of your flesh end? Where do the rules and regulations end? Where does trying to gain God's favor end? It ends up in more than six hundred ways to try to please God.

Jesus closed His lesson to us with these words: "The Son of Man has come to save that which was lost" (Matthew 18:11). Our Lord is telling us, "You can't save yourself. That's why I came. Your salvation is My work alone."

Have you come to the place where you have finally given up all dependence on your own flesh? Have you said, "Lord, I know I can't handle it; this hand, this eye, this foot of mine has taken control of everything"?

If you are still living under the bondage of the Old Covenant, you must repent and confess: "Jesus, I'm not in control anymore. I have messed up everything I have put my hand to. I ask now that Your Holy Spirit take away anything evil that has become rooted in my thinking. Remove all of my offending lusts and habits in the members of my body—my own fleshly ways of trying to please You."

Jesus made it easy for you. Simply place childlike trust in His finished work of the cross. His covenant promises and provisions are found only there.

DISCUSSION QUESTIONS

1. The basic tenet of the Christian faith is that the cross of Jesus Christ accomplished what? (Page 45)

2. Define legalism within the early Church. (Pages 45–46)

3. What was the apostle Paul's response to the demands of the legalists that all believers had to submit to circumcision? (Page 46)

4. List several Scripture passages that Paul gave to the early Church to support his position about circumcision and the Law. (Pages 46, 48)

5. Define what Paul meant when he spoke of the offense of the cross. (Page 47)

6. In Matthew 18:3–5 Jesus gave a profound illustration about children. What was His main point in this teaching? (Page 52)

7. When Jesus spoke of the need to become as little children, what was He speaking of? (Page 52)

8. When Jesus gave a warning to those who would offend little children (those newly converted), whom was He speaking to? Summarize His warning. (Page 55)

9. In Matthew 18:8 Jesus said, "If your hand or foot causes you to sin, cut it off." What was He referring to? (Page 58)

4

ENTERING THE NEW COVENANT
BY DEATH TO SELF

It is a wonderful truth of the New Covenant that the Lord longs for His children to come closer to Him. In fact, He can never get us as close to Him as He desires. He continually unites and binds and fashions us to draw us nearer. As we lay down our vain attempts to earn salvation through our own efforts and embrace the saving work of the cross, our new life within the covenant begins.

The New Covenant, as I have noted, is a binding contract between Father and Son. God sent His Son to redeem a lost world, and Jesus fulfilled His mission through the cross. Since every believer is one with Christ through faith, we are also partners in the contract. This means that we, too, have an obligation. As God draws us closer, our response, our requirement within the contract, is obedience. The burden to obey God in all things is binding upon us.

The question then becomes, How can we ever hope to achieve a life of obedience, a life that is not dominated by sin?

You will recall that in forming the New Covenant, *God promised on oath to supply all the enabling power and strength we need to fulfill every condition and demand of the New Covenant*. So, when God says by oath, "I will do it," faith in us responds, "Let it be so."

Just as God made a way for our salvation through the cross of Christ, He makes a way for us to take up our crosses and walk in this new life. The New Covenant is all about our Lord's commitment to keep His children from falling, and to console, comfort and assure us that the power and dominion of sin can and will be broken by the Holy Spirit who indwells us.

The Holy Spirit will supply all the resources we need. This truth is the sole hope for those believers who have lost heart in their struggle to walk in obedience. Only by having the New Covenant unveiled to us can we learn the secret to having victory over sin.

LESSONS FROM THE DEPTHS

I had yearned for years to understand the New Covenant, believing it could prove to be the wondrous truth that is able to deliver a sin-bound Church in these last days of unprecedented corruption. I pursued this truth diligently, reading every book on the subject I could find, but they were all too technical and mysterious. I wanted to see and experience the power of the New Covenant in my own life. If it is truly the secret of power over the dominion of sin, it had to work in a practical way in my own struggle for purity of heart. I told God that if it did not work in my own life, I could never preach it to others.

So I offered my life and ministry to the Lord as a kind of spiritual laboratory in which to test and prove the truths He was showing me. Now I can tell you, His unveiling of the New Covenant to me has been the most life-giving, sin-destroying truth I have ever known and experienced.

For years, since the day God promised to reveal to me the truth of the covenant, I had been praying, "Lord, when will You open to me its meaning?"

He answered, *You must experience the cross before you can understand it. The doctrine of the New Covenant and your understanding of it will come only after you go through the process of taking up your cross and dying to all that is of self.*

I do not believe we can truly understand the New Covenant until we have gone down into the depths of what it means to die with Christ. I have always known the details of the cross of Christ. Ever since I was a young minister, I preached the cross in vivid pictures. I spoke with sincerity about the sadness of Jesus when He heard of Peter's denial, the crown of thorns pressed into His skull, the mockers, the taunting cries of the mobs, the nails piercing His hands, the sword in His side. I preached passionately, taking the people from the Garden kiss of Judas to the final cry, "It is finished!" But all of that detail—including the pathos of the Calvary scene—is not the deepest meaning of the cross. Most of us know about the physical episode of Calvary—but few have experienced and understood the real spiritual meaning of the crucifixion of Christ, let alone our personal cross and what it means to die with Him.

Jesus had crowds following Him everywhere He went. On one occasion, He stopped suddenly, turned to the masses and said, "You can't be My disciples unless you take up your cross and follow Me" (see Luke 14:27). Many believers have heard this phrase all their lives: *Take up your cross and follow Me.* We read Jesus' words, "He who does not take his cross and follow after Me is not worthy of Me" (Matthew 10:38). "If anyone desires to come after Me, let him deny himself, and take up his cross, and follow Me" (Matthew 16:24). Then Paul declared, "But God forbid that I should boast (glory, KJV) except in the cross of our Lord Jesus Christ, by whom the world has been crucified to me, and I to the world" (Galatians 6:14).

Here is the issue: I cannot be Christ's disciple unless I take up my cross. I cannot obey Him unless it is by the way of the cross. I am not worthy to be His child except by embracing the cross. I am called to glory in the cross. Obviously, it is the key to understanding the New Covenant. But how can I take up the cross, embrace it and yield to it, if I do not know what it means?

TAKING UP THE CROSS

How many definitions of the cross have you heard in your lifetime? I freely admit that for many years I never had the cross shown to me in a way that satisfied my deepest longings about it. I could not preach its fullness because I had not experienced it. And theologically it remained a mystery to me.

In desperation I challenged the Lord, "Father, You know I'm anxious and willing to take up my cross and follow You. But where is it? And what is it? You say it is my cross. And Paul said I must be crucified, I must die. But, Lord, how can You call me to embrace a cross I don't understand? And if I don't understand it, how will I ever come into the knowledge of the New Covenant?"

Answer honestly: Do you understand the meaning of the cross, your cross, your dying, in a personal way? Can you explain to me what taking up your cross means to you, and what happened as a result of your doing it?

Here is the most prevalent explanation I have heard: The cross is some burden—some disturbing element, some kind of painful yoke—such as a chronic illness or a thorn in the flesh. But that definition does not come close. The cross Jesus is talking about is much deeper and darker than all of that. I have heard people say, "Her cross is her wicked, cursing husband." Or, "He hasn't had a day free of pain in twenty years. That's his cross." No—the cross is much more than all of these things.

I am not going to tell you what I know doctrinally about the cross, but I will share with you what I have experienced of the cross. (I am still working on the theology of it all; that will come.) What I am about to share may not make sense to many, but perhaps those who struggle for freedom in their own strength will understand it. Here is my experience of the cross.

DOWN INTO NOTHINGNESS

I experienced the "going down into nothingness." Now, I am not interested in the dictionary's definition of *nothingness*. All I know is that I came to the end of myself—down, down, down into a place of total helplessness.

I had struggled long and hard to be obedient to the Lord, striving earnestly to live a holy life and to be pure. I had tried diligently to beat down every passion and lust in my body and mind. I had read many books and listened to many teachers, looking for keys, insights, secrets to living the life of an overcomer. I had wept until there were no more tears. I had walked and prayed, I had knelt and prayed, I had lain on my face and prayed. I had read my Bible until my eyes were weary. I had begged the Holy Spirit to cut off my offending right arm, pluck out my offending right eye, do whatever He had to do to rid me of all besetting sins. I wanted to be a pleasure to my Lord so badly.

Then one day I could take it no more. On that day, I could not even pray. All I could do was lie on the floor, empty in spirit, with no tears left. Engulfed in a sense of failure, I could only say, "Lord, I cannot go on like this anymore. I am worn out. I have tried and failed. After all my searching through books, all my study, all my efforts to be a conqueror, I still battle with the flesh. My temptations have not let up. I have tried to be a living sacrifice. I have struggled to live by faith. I have tried diligently to live and walk in the Spirit, to allow Him to lead me and empower me. But I still don't get it. I still don't understand why it's not getting through to me."

Down into nothingness I went—where the cry is, "Lord, I can't struggle anymore. I have nothing in me to offer You—no merit, no plea. I have no more power, no more fight. I am weak, helpless. I'm clueless as to what I need to do."

Down to nothingness—where you know nobody on this earth can help you. No counselor, no loved one, no friend, no minister. It is a place where you know that unless the Lord comes to change you—to open your eyes and show you the way—it cannot be done. It is a place where you know beyond any shadow of a doubt you can do nothing on your own. It is where you once and for all face the truth that all your struggling and striving in the flesh have gotten you nowhere, and now everything depends on Him. If there is going to be revelation, He has to give it. If there is going to be deliverance from besetting sins, the Holy Spirit has to do it. If things in my life need fixing, He has to fix them. If I am to be a blessing and joy to Him, He has to make it happen. If I am to walk in the Spirit, He has to show me how. If the Holy Spirit is to empower me to defeat lust or passion, it must happen by imputed faith alone. I am now out of the picture. Out of nothingness must come His supernatural strength. My promises are worthless because I cannot keep any of them. My striving is in vain because I have nothing to work with.

Down to nothingness—where I no longer have a will of my own. On my own I am helpless, "will-less." I have given up my will because it has failed to accomplish any spirituality in me at all. At this place, I found myself on solid ground to remind Jesus that He Himself could do nothing on His own.

> Then Jesus answered and said to them, "Most assuredly, I say to you, the Son can do nothing of Himself, but what He sees the Father do; for whatever He does, the Son also does in like manner. For the Father loves the Son, and shows Him all things that He Himself does; and He will show Him greater works than these, that you may marvel. . . . I can of Myself do nothing. As I hear, I judge; and My judgment is righteous, because I do not seek My own will but the will of the Father who sent Me."
>
> John 5:19–20, 30

It was there in my nothingness that I told Jesus, "You were God in flesh, yet You needed the Father's direction. You could do nothing on Your own. How could You expect any more of me? If You needed help and direction with every step, how much more do I need You to guide me in everything? How much more helpless am I without the same love and guidance from the Father? Jesus, You said Your Father loved You, and, therefore, He showed You 'all things that He Himself does.'"

If I am in Christ, and His Father is my Father, then I am also loved. And He must show me all that He wants to do through me, for Him.

Then said Jesus to them, "When you lift up the Son of Man, then you will know that I am He, and that I do nothing of Myself; but as My Father taught Me, I speak these things. And He who sent Me is with Me. The Father has not left Me alone, for I always do those things that please Him."

John 8:28–29

Nothingness—a place where you feel abandoned. You love Him, you desire Him, you know that He is, but you feel that for some unknown reason He is silent. His revelation is not coming to you. He is not answering your heart's cry for a clearer vision of what you are going through.

In such an hour, Jesus cried to the Father, "'Eloi, Eloi, lama sabachthani?' which is translated, 'My God, My God, why have You forsaken Me?'" (Mark 15:34). I made the same cry: "Father, all I want is to do Your will and please You. Why must I bear this sense that I'm on my own? Why do You not respond in my desperate time? Why is my soul so cast down with feelings of rejection and confusion?"

BREAKING THROUGH THE CLOUDS

When Jesus said to His followers, "Take up your cross and follow Me," He meant, "You will go down the same path to death." A cross experience is when you think God has turned a deaf ear to your cry for righteousness and holiness. For a season your prayers go unanswered, and your heart rises up and begins to reason: "All I wanted was to be like Jesus—to walk in victory, to be a joy to Him, to enjoy sweet communion. But this? Why is there no clear way, no reassurance? Why is this darkness in my soul—this feeling of speaking into God's ear, yet He appears not to hear? Why does it have to be so complicated?"

It is at this point in His crucifixion that Jesus broke through the devil's cloud and cried aloud in faith. "When Jesus had cried out with a loud voice, He said, 'Father, into Your hands I commit My spirit.' Having said this, He breathed His last" (Luke 23:46).

Here is where the cross is most powerfully experienced. It happens when in my nothingness, I surrender my will—I quit struggling and striving. I now become wholly dependent on Him. The matter is now out of my hands completely; God has to take over. His Spirit must take me into death and raise me up as a new man. I give up the ghost, the independent life of flesh. Death to all ambition. Death to boasting and trying to impress others. Death to doing anything on my own. Death to my plans, desires, will. Death to all my striving to please Him. And, most of all, death to my past flesh-faith.

How many times have I struggled to muster up faith and tried to pump it up with promises? I repeated over and over, "Lord, I believe, I do believe, I really believe. I really, truly, honestly believe." But it did not work. (You can always tell a request that is of the flesh, because it comes with a deadline. We give God what we consider long enough to act—but when He does not perform on schedule, our so-called faith turns into ugly unbelief.)

Death—it is the only way out of the Old Covenant and into the New. "Flesh-faith" has to die. No more striving to believe. If I am to have faith—true faith, the faith of Christ—He has to give it to me. We have been given a measure of faith—yet if it is true that I can do nothing of myself, then this includes having His faith. That is why Scripture calls it "the faith of Christ."

Paul wrote:

I was alive once without the law, but when the commandment came, sin revived and I died. And the commandment, which was

I, a licensed, ordained Baptist minister, was also addicted—a slave to my own efforts of salvation.

I have spent the better part of my life working to help people get free from life-controlling addictions, including every type of drug imaginable. Running a Christian recovery home, I have had to deal with heroin and cocaine addicts, alcoholics and the latest scourge of addiction, methamphetamine. As a professional social worker I have seen the damage that addiction wreaks on families. Everyone around an addict ends up strangling, dying slowly, one broken promise at a time.

After more than 25 years I thought I had seen all the tricks and traps of addiction and witnessed all the death she had to deal until one day through Brother Dave's teaching on the New Covenant, I discovered that I, an ordained minister, was also addicted—a slave to my own efforts of salvation.

Understanding this teaching was like putting a mirror before my own religious masks. I had been tricked into trying on different masks that left me "powerless over my addiction." I had tried all that my addiction had to offer: rules, rituals, religious fervor and stoicism. Ultimately, like any true addict, I failed them all and hid my failure and rejection in even more religion.

I had read all of Brother Dave's books and heard him preach a hundred sermons, and they had been medicine to my selfish, sickly heart. But ultimately no book or sermon could undo the bonds of a religion based on self. I was trapped in a web of my own spinning, and the face on the spider was mine.

Comprehending the New Covenant was at once an arrow through my heart and the transplant of a new one. Yes, I was saved. I had been saved since I was a boy, but like most other preachers I know, I would be up, then down, then tossed to and fro. It took a lot of effort and time just to stay afloat. The epiphany for me came when I learned that I didn't have to struggle or swim—but, safe in Christ, led by the Holy Spirit, I could float.

My life changed when I learned that. My preaching changed. And the greatest thing about it was I really didn't have a thing to do with it, nor did I need to do anything to keep it going. When Christ said, "It is finished" on the cross, it was!

—Rick

to bring life, I found to bring death. For sin, taking occasion by the commandment, deceived me, and by it killed me. Therefore the law is holy, and the commandment holy and just and good. Has then what is good become death to me? Certainly not! But sin, that it might appear sin, was producing death in me through what is good, so that sin through the commandment might become exceedingly sinful.

Romans 7:9–13

Are you sin-sick? Are you truly yearning to live a holy life, free from the habituating lusts of the flesh? Then get ready to die. Get ready to embrace the cross. The Old Covenant will bring you to your wits' end—to nothingness. When you have given up all hope of overcoming sin by your own human power and will, then you are ready to enter the glorious realm of freedom through the New Covenant.

DISCUSSION QUESTIONS

1. The New Covenant is about the Lord's commitment to keep His children from the power and dominion of sin by what means? (Page 62)

2. What is the secret to having total victory over sin? (Page 62)

3. Read Matthew 10:38. We cannot be Christ's disciples unless what happens? (Page 64)

4. Do you understand the meaning of "the cross" and "your cross"? In your own words explain what this means. (Page 65)

5. What do you think the phrase *down into nothing-ness* means? (Pages 66–67)

6. Where is the cross most powerfully experienced? (Page 69)

7. The only way out of the Old Covenant and into the New Covenant is through what? (Page 69)

5

THE NEW COVENANT AND THE INDWELLING HOLY SPIRIT

In this chapter, I want to show you the need for the indwelling power of the Holy Spirit. And I must emphasize again that no one in his own strength is able to live an overcoming life, free from sin's power and dominion. He may grieve over his sins, shedding a river of tears, but in his own willpower and ability he cannot defeat powerful, besetting sins.

When the prophet Ezekiel preached repentance to the nation of Israel, he knew that God was grieved over Israel's backsliding and compromise. He told the people:

> "Repent, and turn from all your transgressions, so that iniquity will not be your ruin. Cast away from you all the transgressions which you have committed, and get yourselves a new heart and a new spirit. . . . Therefore, turn and live!"
>
> Ezekiel 18:30–32

They were being told, in essence, "You know what you are doing is wrong, so why don't you stop it? Lay it down. Just say no to your besetting sin. Turn from it, and make a change in yourself. Get yourself a new heart."

Ezekiel himself enjoyed the overcoming power of the Holy Spirit in his life. He was one of a number of Old Testament prophets whose holy lives were due solely to the indwelling presence of God's Spirit. All through Old Covenant times, we read of certain people who were touched by the Holy Spirit and filled with His presence. The Spirit Himself gave them the inner resources they needed to resist temptation and overcome sin. Though the Spirit had not been outpoured, God in His mercy gave the Spirit to those who had been called to some great work.

And so it was with Ezekiel. He experienced the Holy Spirit's indwelling power, testifying, "The Spirit entered me when He spoke to me" (Ezekiel 2:2). But Ezekiel's audience knew nothing of their need for the indwelling presence of God's Spirit. They could not overcome their sin no matter how hard they tried.

This baffled the prophet. He could not comprehend why the Israelites did not simply become convicted by God's Word, heed His powerful warnings and turn themselves around. That is why he urged them, "You need to motivate yourselves to turn away from your sin. You need to get yourself a new spirit."

I preached this same Old Covenant message for years, in all sincerity. I grieved over the sins I saw taking place in God's house, and I desperately wanted people to repent and turn from their wickedness. So I preached, in so many words, "Why are you letting your sins ruin you? Why are you allowing yourself to be continually bound and fettered by your lusts? You need to walk away from them. Just do it! Get mad at the devil. Don't take any more from him. Cast off your iniquity and turn yourself around. You know God hates it—so stop it before it destroys you. Get yourself a new heart for Jesus."

I do not renounce any of those past messages. I believe such preaching has a purpose, because it makes people realize their impotence to stop sinning, and produces in them a crisis that drives them to the cross. It is God's Law being held up as a mirror to reveal the exceeding sinfulness of sin.

The problem was, however, that I was asking people to do something humanly impossible. I have numerous books in my library on the subject of holiness and sanctification. They are convicting, and they all say the same thing: God demands holiness, purity and obedience. They warn of the consequences of continuing in sin, and they clearly define the commands of Christ. They say, essentially, "Here is what is demanded of you. And here is what will happen if you don't shape up."

But these books do not tell us how to obtain the power and authority to obey. Over the years I read many of these books without understanding God's New Covenant provisions. This served only to add to my burden of guilt and condemnation. The message to "just do it" is impossible.

And it was just as impossible in Ezekiel's day. The children of Israel had none of the power they needed to turn themselves from sin and cast off their iniquity. They could no more create in themselves a new heart than they could raise the dead. This was the central problem of the Old Covenant. It demanded perfect obedience, a wholehearted turning from sin—but the command was not accompanied by the indwelling power to obey. (This is why God made a New Covenant with humankind.)

Now, I am certain there were believers in Israel who heard Ezekiel's message and hungered for righteousness. After all, there was a holy remnant in Israel during this period. And I believe that when these people heard the prophet's powerful, convicting message, they cried, "That's what I want—a new heart. I want to be set free from the burden and shame of my sin. But I keep failing, Ezekiel. I want to do what you're telling me, but I simply don't have the power within me to accomplish it. I have tried to say no to my sin. I've done everything humanly possible to rid my soul of the dreadful thing that holds me in bondage, but I keep falling back into it. I don't want to reproach God. I don't want this iniquity to ruin my life, but I can't cast out my own sin. I need a new heart that's beyond my ability to create."

The Source of Power

As I have pointed out, under the New Covenant God demands total obedience of His people. He does not wink at sin in these days of grace. He commands us to turn aside from all our iniquities and calls us to have a new heart. But we, like Ezekiel's contemporaries, are helpless to break the dominion of sin through our own strength. Where can we find the needed power?

The psalmist tells us, "The secret of the LORD is with those who fear Him, and He will show them His covenant" (Psalm 25:14). This was true in Ezekiel's day. The prophet was a part of God's holy remnant at the time, walking in righteous fear before the Lord, and God was about to open his eyes to the incredible blessings of the covenant.

Ezekiel must have been distraught over what he saw going on in Israel. God's people were in disarray and the priests were obsessed with their own welfare, piling up wealth for themselves. They cheated the people and lived off the fat of the offerings while the populace suffered. People wandered about everywhere looking for spiritual food, with no shepherds to feed them, lead them or bind their wounds.

Moreover, Scripture says, the Israelites were still living in sin and trusting in their own righteousness. God told Ezekiel, "They hear your words, but they do not do them; for with their mouth they show much love, but their hearts pursue their own gain. . . . They hear your words, but they do not do them" (Ezekiel 33:31–32).

In this dark, hopeless hour, God shared with Ezekiel a great mystery. He was about to lift Ezekiel out of his Old Covenant surroundings and reveal to him a glorious work that would take place in the time of the Messiah. God was going to unveil the New Covenant for him.

Suddenly, the prophet's mouth was filled with the word of the Lord. Immediately Ezekiel began preaching a message that must have both thrilled and dumbfounded him. God spoke through him:

> "Then I will sprinkle clean water on you, and you shall be clean; I will cleanse you from all your filthiness and from all your idols. I will give you a new heart and put a new spirit within you; I will take the heart of stone out of your flesh and give you a heart of flesh. I will put My Spirit within you and cause you to walk in My statutes, and you will keep My judgments and do them."
>
> Ezekiel 36:25–27

This message was almost too good to be true. God was saying, "I am going to put My very own Spirit in sin-bound people, and My Spirit will cause them to fulfill every command I have ever given them. They have come to the end of themselves, Ezekiel. They are dead to any ability to overcome. But My Spirit is going to empower them to turn away from their sin."

What a glorious word! Yet Ezekiel must have wondered, "Lord, did I hear You correctly? I've been telling the people to clean themselves up and get a new heart. But now You're saying the day is coming when You will do it for them, by Your Spirit. Are You really going to cleanse them—to take away all the filth from their lives? And will You really give them a new heart, *and cause them to obey You*—all by Your mercy alone? Can this be true?"

CAN DRY BONES LIVE?

To prove what He had just promised, God used a vision, taking Ezekiel into a valley full of dry bones, where He gave him an illustrated sermon. This was an astonishing revelation of a New Covenant promise.

> The hand of the LORD came upon me and brought me out in the Spirit of the LORD, and set me down in the midst of the valley; and it was full of bones. Then He caused me to pass by them all around, and behold, there were very many in the open valley; and indeed they were very dry.
>
> Ezekiel 37:1–2

After God showed Ezekiel this valley full of dry bones, He asked the prophet, "Son of man, can these bones live?" (verse 3). By posing this question, the Lord was saying something significant. He was telling Ezekiel, "These bones represent your people. They are dry, bleached out, crumbling, with no life whatsoever. Ezekiel, you've been preaching to a dead congregation.

"You can preach to them all you want about turning from sin and getting a new heart," God was saying. "You can tell them how their sin has killed them, how they need to get up and walk in new life. But, I ask you, Ezekiel, can these dry bones do that? Can they make themselves come to life and heed your words? Can they suddenly get up out of their graves just because you have preached a convicting message to them? Can dead people resurrect themselves? Under the Old Covenant it is impossible."

Beloved, God is asking the same question of every Gospel preacher today. He is telling us, "Stop trying to get dead people to obey Me. Quit trying to produce holiness in dead men by commanding them to get up out of their graves. Can lifeless corpses do what you ask of them?"

I spent years preaching to dead, dry bones. I would scream to the lifeless believers in front of me, "Why are you letting your sin ruin and destroy you? Get up out of your grave of iniquity and walk in holiness." Yet if their spirits could have talked, they would have answered, "I can't, Preacher. Can't you see I'm dead? I don't have any power to do what you're asking, because there is no life in me."

I said they were believers yet dead. How could that be, if no one can be saved unless the Holy Spirit is at work in him? The death I speak of is the one Paul describes in Romans 7—the death that falls upon all believers who try to gain merit with God through works. Paul writes, "I was alive once without the law, but when the commandment came, sin revived and I died. . . . For sin, taking occasion by the commandment, deceived me, and by it killed me" (Romans 7:9, 11). In other words: "When I preached holiness and separation without the power of the New Covenant, I was hurrying a sinful people on toward a much-needed death. By my urging them to try harder to keep the commandments in purity, they soon realized they were helpless to obey in their own strength."

"Having died to what we were held by . . ." (verse 6). Paul is telling us, "The Law was good but impossible to keep. It showed me how exceedingly sinful I am. What was meant for good brought me to death." All believers who serve God under the Old Covenant of works as merit are still dead, meaning helpless to please God and obey Him. They are absolutely powerless. That is why we so desperately need to understand the need of the Holy Spirit to indwell us.

At this point, Ezekiel's vision of the indwelling Spirit had already informed him about the new work God was going to do through the Holy Spirit. And now the Lord was opening Ezekiel's eyes fully. He told him, in essence, "Ezekiel, the only way these dry bones are ever going to live to obey Me is if My Spirit enters them and does the work. It can happen only by the indwelling of the Holy Spirit."

God then instructed Ezekiel to preach the following:

> "O dry bones, hear the word of the LORD! Thus says the Lord GOD to these bones: 'Surely I will cause breath to enter into you, and you shall live. I will put sinews on you and bring flesh upon you, cover you with skin and put breath in you; and you shall live. Then you shall know that I am the LORD.'"
>
> Ezekiel 37:4–6

What followed was a supernatural work of God. First, there was a mighty shaking, accompanied by a lot of noise. Then, suddenly, Ezekiel saw all the dry bones coming together on the ground to form bodies. In the next instant, flesh appeared on those bones. What an amazing sight! *God was raising up lifeless bones, to prepare them as vessels to be filled with His Spirit.*

Without knowing it, Ezekiel was preaching the New Covenant message. He was saying, "All you dead men and women—hear the Lord. The only way you are going to defeat the sin that has ruined your life is if God's Spirit does the work in you. He has to enter in and take dominion. Only He can bring you to life so that you can obey God."

This message is at the very heart of the New Covenant. Simply put, God's Spirit will accomplish in us what our flesh has never been able to do. How? By indwelling us. The New Covenant is all about the Holy Spirit coming to live and work in us, by promise in answer to faith.

LAYING HOLD OF THE PROMISE

What is the point of this lesson Ezekiel learned? What is the Holy Spirit teaching us? This passage reveals God's desire for us to lay hold of the promises of His New Covenant. It is about truly learning how to live—by entering into the blessings of the covenant.

These vessels lying lifeless on the ground were prepared and ready. As we read above, the Lord had told them, "O dry bones, hear the word of the LORD!" (Ezekiel 37:4). They had heard God's covenant promise: "I will put My Spirit in you, and you shall live."

Yet, even though these dead bones had had the New Covenant promises preached to them, they had not yet entered into the enjoyment of its blessings. They now had flesh on them, but they still lay lifeless on the ground. They must have looked like store mannequins—with eyes, hair, color in their cheeks. But they were still corpses.

I believe God is telling us in this passage, "You can hear about all the glorious blessings of My New Covenant—all My promises to put My very own Spirit in you, to empower you to obey Me in all things, to give you a new heart, to cause you to know Me. You can live totally under My covenant in the time of its fulfillment. You can testify to an initial work of the Spirit in you. And yet you still might not enjoy the power and freedom given to you through this covenant."

Indeed, many believers today know of God's New Covenant— yet they can hardly believe it, because it sounds too good to be true. They say, "I know God has given His people the Holy Spirit to come and indwell us. And I know the Spirit takes it upon Himself to cause us to obey Christ. Oh, I want that blessing badly, but how can I lay hold of it? How can I obtain it for my life?"

There is something we must do. Ezekiel writes:

> Also He said to me, "Prophesy to the breath, prophesy, son of man, and say to the breath, 'Thus says the Lord GOD: "Come from the four winds, O breath, and breathe on these slain, that they may live."'" So I prophesied as He commanded me, and breath came into them, and they lived, and stood upon their feet, an exceedingly great army.
>
> Ezekiel 37:9–10

Suddenly there stood before Ezekiel a great army, alive and breathing. The Holy Spirit had filled all those dead bodies with life—and now they were prepared to do battle. In an instant they had entered into the full enjoyment and blessings of the New Covenant. God's Spirit had taken His rightful place in them—and He was bringing about all the promised changes.

What made the Holy Spirit come in and respond to the need, bringing these dry bones into the blessings of the New Covenant? Jesus tells us clearly, "If you . . . know how to give good gifts to your children, how much more will your heavenly Father give the Holy Spirit to those who ask Him!" (Luke 11:13). Scripture also makes it clear that there is a right way to ask for the Holy Spirit.

In Ezekiel's case, he was not merely to pray, "Come, Holy Spirit, fill these dry bones with life again." No—God instructed the prophet specifically: "Prophesy to the breath [His Spirit] . . . 'Thus says the Lord GOD: . . . "Breathe on these slain, that they may live."'"

The Lord was telling Ezekiel, "Speak to the Holy Spirit, Ezekiel. Tell Him, 'Thus saith the Lord, "Bring life."' Remind Him of the covenant promises. State them to Him as My sworn Word to you." Ezekiel had first prophesied to the bones—but now he was being instructed to prophesy, or preach, *to the Holy Spirit.*

Ezekiel was being directed to challenge the Holy Spirit with the promises of God's covenant. He was to say to the Spirit, "It is written—God has promised me on oath that He would send You to indwell me. You, Holy Spirit, inspired holy men to record these glorious promises. You promised to take full possession of my new heart, according to Your own inspired Word. And You are to cause me to walk in holiness—to empower me to obey all His commands. So I say to You, Holy Spirit, with all respect—You are under oath to fulfill that promise. I hold You to Your own Word. I lay hold of Your promises by faith. This is the Word of almighty God—and I commit my soul to it."

If Release Is Blocked

The apostle Paul wrote in the New Testament: "If you live according to the flesh you will die; but if by the Spirit you put to death the deeds of the body, you will live" (Romans 8:13). Paul did not speak these words to dry bones, but to living, breathing believers. Yet he implied that they did not have true life if sin still had dominion over them. He was saying, "If you remain under the power of sin, you're not really living. You're dead inside—converted, but not really living. And you will stay that way until your besetting sin is gone. You simply cannot know the meaning of life until God's Spirit mortifies your sin."

Perhaps you feel like these believers Paul addressed. You may object, "But, Brother Dave, I know the Holy Spirit lives in me.

He has filled me and baptized me, making my body His temple. So, if He has promised to cause me to forsake all sin and obey His Word, why don't I see His power at work? Here I am, a lover of Jesus, a supposedly Spirit-filled believer, but I'm still not totally free from the dominion of sin. I feel helpless in my struggle to walk uprightly before Him. What's my problem?"

Over the years I have ministered to many such God-hungry saints, including pastors. Their one great desire is to live righteously and purely before the Lord. Yet they struggle with some kind of besetting sin—perhaps a bad temper, or covetousness, or fear of man, or bitterness, or jealousy, or lust. These people tell me, "I know God's Spirit abides in me, but I can't find the release of power I need to overcome my sin. Tell me—if God's Spirit dwells in me, then where is His power? Why isn't it coming out in me? It's almost as if the Holy Spirit is bottled up in me somehow."

I believe if a Christian intensely desires a holy life—if he longs to give his all to the Lord—there can be only one reason why he fails to enjoy the blessing and freedom promised by the indwelling of the Holy Spirit. That reason is unbelief.

Unblocking Unbelief

As surely as Jesus could not perform His works when He encountered unbelief, so His Spirit cannot do anything in our lives when we harbor unbelief.

It is vital for every follower of Jesus not to judge God's New Covenant promises according to past experiences. If we cast ourselves fully on His covenant promises—believing them with all our being, trusting Him for a supply of faith, holding the Spirit to His own Word—then we can know the results are all

Only when the Christian heart grasps the magnitude of the finished work of Calvary will we understand the magnitude of the command to be free from sin.

"It is finished!" These words have stuck with me since I got hold of what the New Covenant really means in my life. Jesus said, "When the Son of Man comes, will He really find faith on the earth?" (Luke 18:8). I believe there is a close relationship between Jesus' question and His declaration that "It is finished."

It has been my privilege to work with men and women struggling with homosexuality. I came from such a background, and I truly believe there is no cure for people caught in such a sin, nor is there healing from its wounds or deliverance from its bondage, aside from the power of the shed blood of Christ. I have never seen a clever counseling method or a "secret wisdom" that has brought relief. I have seen the power of the Holy Spirit bring relief, however, when the truth of the Gospel takes root in a person's heart. Where there was defeat, there comes a fight, yes, but that fight begins in Christ's victorious proclamation that "It is finished!" Then these men and women do find victory.

The finished work of Calvary is the premise from which every promise has been set in motion for the Christian. It declares every debt paid, sin dealt with, sickness healed and "darkness swallowed up in victory." It affords us the power of the Holy Spirit as this "corruptible must put on incorruption, and this mortal must put on immortality" (1 Corinthians 15:53).

It is not until we hear and understand this truth that we gain power in Christ and have faith to overcome. We hear the words of the Father, "This is My beloved Son, in whom I am well pleased," and know that we are "accepted in the beloved," sharing this affection with the Father in fellowship with Christ. We are no longer orphans, but accepted because of the New Covenant.

By His grace I walk in freedom today, and I have found "rest for my weary soul."

—Dez

God's responsibility. And we will be able to stand on Judgment Day, having been faithful. We simply cannot give up our desire to enter into His promised blessings.

There was a point in my life when I cast my eternal future on God's covenant promises. I determined to trust His covenant oath at the risk of my very soul. I put out this challenge to almighty God: "Lord, I'm going to believe You have given me Your Holy Spirit. I believe He alone can deliver me from every chain that binds me. I believe He will convict me, lead me and empower me to overcome. I believe He causes me to obey Your Word, and I believe He will never depart from me, nor will He let me depart from You. I will not limit Your Spirit in me. I will wait on Him, call on Him and trust in Him—live or die."

We must do what the Lord told Ezekiel to do: Pray the covenant. We are instructed to remind the Holy Spirit of God's promises to us. We are to tell Him: "Holy Spirit, the heavenly Father promised me He would put You in my heart, and I have committed myself to that promise. I will yield and I will cooperate, for I want to be holy. You said You will cause me to walk in His ways and obey His every word. I don't know how You plan to do that, but You made an oath, and You cannot lie. This is all written in the Word, Holy Spirit. So, come—do Your work in me. I entrust my very soul to this promise."

THE PROMISES ARE OURS

The Bible makes it clear that Ezekiel's vision was not about his own day, but the coming day of the Messiah—the very day we live in now. God had told the prophet, "These bones are the whole house of Israel" (Ezekiel 37:11). Ezekiel knew God was speaking not of natural Israel but of spiritual Israel. King David had long been dead by Ezekiel's day. So, when Ezekiel prophesied about David, it is clear he was speaking of the promised seed of David—the coming Messiah, Jesus Christ:

> "David My servant shall be king over them, and they shall all have one shepherd; they shall also walk in My judgments and observe My statutes, and do them. . . . And My servant David shall be their prince forever."
>
> Ezekiel 37:24–25

Think about it for a moment: None of these prophecies has yet been fulfilled in natural Israel. That nation has never had a prince forever or a shepherd who ruled over the people continuously. No, Ezekiel was speaking of an eternal Kingdom—one under the rule of Christ, the great Shepherd.

Now, you may object, "But what about the promise in verse fourteen of that chapter? It says, 'I will put My Spirit in you, and you shall live, and I will place you in your own land.' Isn't it clear that this promise can only be about natural Israel, because it is a specific place with its own land?"

No, not at all. The Hebrew word for *land* here suggests "solid ground, a place of firmness, unshakable." God is saying in this passage, "I am going to bring you to a place of absolute firmness in your faith. It will be solid ground, where nothing can shake your spirit."

Ezekiel understood this. In fact, he surely knew the prophecy Isaiah had given more than a hundred years earlier about the land that God was bringing His people into:

> You shall no longer be termed Forsaken, nor shall your land any more be termed Desolate; but you shall be called Hephzibah,

and your land Beulah; for the LORD delights in you, and your land shall be married.

Isaiah 62:4

The name *Beulah* here means "a wife whose husband is her master." It also means "my delight is in her." This passage is obviously referring to the redeemed Church, under the lordship of Christ.

Today, according to God's covenant, every true believer in Jesus Christ stands on a firm, unshakable place under the full control of the Master. We cannot bring ourselves under Him; we have to rely on the Holy Spirit to do that work. The Spirit is the One who says, "I'm bringing you into Beulah land—to live under the authority of your Master, Jesus, and to fulfill all His desires."

We live in that day when the Prince is ruling—when there is one Shepherd over the people, Jesus. The Holy Spirit is even now bringing a host into His Beulah land of promise. And it is a place of firmness because it sits on the bedrock that is Christ. In this land, we are no longer prey to demon powers. God's Word tells us, "You are never again going to be a victim of the devil. Now you have the fullness of My Spirit at work in you."

"'Therefore I will save My flock, and they shall no longer be a prey. . . . I will establish one shepherd over them, and he shall feed them—My servant David. . . . I, the LORD, will be their God, and My servant David a prince among them. . . . I will make a covenant of peace with them, and cause wild beasts to cease from the land; and they will dwell safely in the wilderness and sleep in the woods. . . . They shall no longer be a prey for the nations, nor shall beasts of the land devour them; but they shall dwell safely, and no one shall make them afraid. . . . Thus they shall know that I, the LORD their God, am with them, and they, the house of Israel, are My people,' says the Lord GOD."

Ezekiel 34:22–25, 28, 30

Our Lord has given us this "covenant of peace" by driving out all the evil beasts in our lives. All the old ghosts, all the nagging thoughts, all the memories of sin that once haunted us are gone now. We have been set free to focus on the victory of the cross—and on the indwelling power of the Holy Spirit.

DISCUSSION QUESTIONS

1. What was the prophet stressing in Ezekiel 18:30–32? (Page 74)

2. What is the central problem of the Old Covenant? (Page 75)

3. If we are helpless to break the dominion of sin through our own strength, where can we find the needed power? (Page 76)

4. God unveiled the New Covenant to the prophet in Ezekiel 36:25–27. What was the heart of this message? (Page 77)

5. The valley of dry bones that the prophet saw represented what? (Page 78)

6. When God instructed Ezekiel to preach to the dry bones, what was the central message he was to proclaim? (Page 80)

7. What is the Holy Spirit teaching us about the New Covenant through Ezekiel 37? (Page 80)

8. How did Ezekiel prompt the Holy Spirit to come and bring the dry bones into the blessing of the New Covenant? (Page 83)

9. What does unbelief do to the working of the Holy Spirit in your life? (Page 84)

10. The promises of the New Covenant would not come in Ezekiel's day. When would the fulfillment come? (Page 86)

6

THE NEW COVENANT
AND THE FEAR OF GOD

I believe that God has to accomplish a certain work in us before we can lay claim to any covenant promise. What is this
precedent work upon which all others depend? The prophet
Jeremiah tells us: "I will put My fear in their hearts so that they
will not depart from Me" (Jeremiah 32:40). God's precedent
work of the covenant is to put His fear in our hearts, by the
work of the Holy Spirit.

Jeremiah is speaking here of the provisions of God's New
Covenant, not the Old. God tells us clearly how this first work
of the covenant will be performed: "I will put My fear in their
hearts." He is letting us know we cannot work up a holy fear
by ourselves. We cannot obtain it by the laying on of hands or
the striving of our flesh. No—the only way this holy work can
be accomplished in us is if God's Spirit performs it.

God is telling us through this passage, "I am going to do marvelous things in you. I will send My very own Spirit to you, who will abide in you and give you a new heart. He will empower you to mortify all deeds of the flesh, and He will guide you into total freedom from the power of sin. Finally, He will cause you to will and do My good pleasure.

"But," God says, "there is one work the Spirit must perform in you before any of these others. He is going to put in you the true fear of God concerning sin. He will implant in you a profound awe of My holiness so you will not depart from My commands. Otherwise, your sin will always lead you away from Me."

Very simply, the Holy Spirit changes the way we look at our sin. He knows that as long as we continue to take our lusts lightly, we will never be set free. So He shows us how deeply it grieves and provokes Him. How does the Holy Spirit do this? He uses the convicting Word of God—the piercing arrows of holy truth.

If you are sick of your sin, and you hunger to walk in righteousness, then be prepared: God is going to shoot Gospel arrows of conviction into your heart. You will feel their flames of truth burning deep into your conscience. They will seek out every hidden area, exposing every lust.

Many flesh-driven Christians try to shake off the guilt that God's convicting arrows produce. They do not want to feel the dread of their sin, so they constantly claim the verse, "There is therefore now no condemnation to those who are in Christ Jesus" (Romans 8:1). But they neglect to read the last part of this verse: "who do not walk according to the flesh, but according to the Spirit." If you continue in sin, you are walking in the flesh—and you have no claim on God's promise of "no condemnation."

The guilt we feel under Holy Spirit conviction is actually a work of God's grace. It is meant to expose the deceitfulness of sin in us. We should ask God's Spirit, therefore, to load up our

God has sworn by His own name that He will make us the man and woman He wants us to be—that, despite our shortcomings and failures, He is not taken by surprise.

In our marriage, we have been able to see the best of each other and the worst of each other. Have you been there? Our personal shortcomings are highlighted and magnified thousands of times. Our sinful nature sticks up its ugly head far too many times, and the worst part is that our spouse, the one whom God has entrusted us with, gets the short end of the stick. This takes us far away from that precious goal of being the godly spouse that we are supposed to be. Sometimes, the intensity of the issue is such that it seems impossible to overcome. Will this ever change? Uninvited, depression sneaks in—and hope slowly starts to fade out . . . to pitch black.

The New Covenant shines God's light on this helpless picture, destroying the darkness, strengthening our faith and reviving hope. It reassures us that God has sworn by His own name that *He* will make us the man and woman He wants us to be—that, despite our shortcomings, personal failures and wounds from the past, He is not taken by surprise. He still loves us and He will change us. He has promised that if we ask Him, He will cause us to want new hearts. He will cause us to believe that He is greater than our personal issues and that He will cause us to want His love for each other. He has promised that the tactics and attacks of the enemy will be used to mature our faith in Him and our love for one another. He is bound to change our lives again and again, for the glory of His name.

—*Mr. and Mrs. E.*

consciences continually with the guilt, fear and condemnation of sin, but only until its exceeding sinfulness is completely exposed. It is then that the Spirit of God can redeem us of it all, because it has accomplished its purpose in driving us to His marvelous grace.

THE DANGERS OF SIN

Many Christians are not aware of the terrible danger they are in when they continue in sin. Only the Holy Spirit's flaming arrows of truth can awaken their souls to the godly fear they need in order to shake off sin. Let me share with you a few of the flaming arrows of reality the Lord has used to pierce my soul.

> 1. *God considers hidden lusts and sins in Christians to be as dangerous and hateful to Him as the flagrant sins committed by wicked unbelievers.*

Most believers think their hidden sin is not serious simply because they do not act on it. But God sees into His people's hearts—and in His sight the sin He sees within us outweighs that of wicked sinners.

No doubt, humankind today has seen murders, genocides and flaunted acts of sin beyond that of any previous generation. Yet, here is God's perspective on it all: Nothing compares to the clinging lusts in a believer's heart. Our evil lusts, hatreds and bosom sins are vile in His sight.

We see an example of this perspective in Revelation. God told the Laodicean church, "I know your works, that you are neither cold nor hot" (Revelation 3:15). He is saying, "I know you—and you're not what you profess to be. You tell yourself, 'I'm in need of nothing.' But I say you are getting lukewarm.

The zeal you once had for Me is slowly drying up. Everyone else sees you as an upright, prosperous church, but I see into your heart and I know you are not who you claim to be."

Proverbs tells us, "Out of [the heart] spring the issues of life" (4:23). Likewise, "As [a man] thinks in his heart, so is he" (23:7). These verses are the sharp arrows of the Holy Spirit. They pierce our hearts, telling us, "You can't hide from God's sight. Every secret thing that is hidden in your soul is going to be brought into the open. It doesn't matter if you act on it or not. God will not excuse your secret lusts, your evil thoughts, your clinging bondage to sin."

You are ready for the delivering promises of the New Covenant the moment you sincerely ask the Holy Spirit to put the fear of God in you to never again take sin lightly.

> 2. *The longer we continue in sin, the more we are in danger of hardening our hearts.*

The Bible warns that if we continue in sin, eventually we will become conviction-proof:

> Beware, brethren, lest there be in any of you an evil heart of unbelief in departing from the living God; but exhort one another daily, while it is called "Today," *lest any of you be hardened through the deceitfulness of sin.*
>
> Hebrews 3:12–13, emphasis added

Perhaps at one time you trembled at hearing God's Word. You melted whenever you heard a sermon that you knew was meant especially for you. You had an ear to hear the Spirit's voice. But for some time now, you have been flirting with a bosom sin— toying with it, playing with it, rolling it around in your mind. And now, because sin has worked its deceit in you, you can sit unmoved through any sermon, no matter how anointed it is. You can read God's Word and fellowship with brokenhearted, repentant believers, yet never feel a thing. Your heart can grow cold, until you no longer feel any conviction whatsoever.

If you had the gift of godly fear, it would quickly reveal to you that your heart is slowly but surely growing hard. You would realize that every day you continue indulging in sin, you get closer to having your conscience seared. Day by day, your sin becomes less and less obnoxious to you, and soon you are going to end up blinded, with false peace. Finally, your bosom lust will spill over the boundaries you set for it, and it will flow wildly into every kind of evil act.

I have seen firsthand the horrors befalling a man of God who allowed his heart to grow hard. He was a minister friend of mine who pastored a large church. God blessed this man mightily, anointing his sermons with Holy Spirit fire and power. But the minister harbored a secret sexual lust, and over time he began to indulge it—and eventually he was caught in the act of adultery.

God was merciful to my pastor friend. Godly elders and church leaders disciplined him and in time he was restored to the ministry. At that point, whenever lust arose in his heart, the Holy Spirit was faithful to deal with him about it—but this man never took his sin seriously. Preacher after preacher stood in his pulpit delivering convicting messages on hidden sin. I know, because I was one of those preachers. But that pastor never inclined his heart to hear the Spirit's voice.

I was there the night he was exposed *again*. Five women came forward and confessed to having an affair with him. Some said they even had sexual relations with him just hours before he stepped into the pulpit to preach.

A friend of mine later asked this man, "How could your conscience allow you to do that? How could you conduct an affair with a woman and then rush to the pulpit to preach God's Holy Word?"

The pastor answered with a laugh, "You have to be a good actor."

Beloved, that is a hard heart. Nothing moved this man. He had become so hardened, he could indulge in adultery, open his Bible and preach without a trace of guilt.

Ask the Holy Spirit to accomplish in you the precedent work of instilling godly fear in you, to keep your heart open and accepting of God's Word. When you do, the Spirit promises to give you a soft heart, one that is pliable in His hand.

3. If we continue in sin, we will face the rod of God.

The psalmist wrote the following about one of God's prime covenant promises:

> "If his sons forsake My law and do not walk in My judgments, if they break My statutes and do not keep My commandments, then I will punish their transgression with the rod, and their iniquity with stripes. Nevertheless My lovingkindness I will not utterly take from him, nor allow My faithfulness to fail. My covenant I will not break, nor alter the word that has gone out of My lips."
>
> Psalm 89:30–34

We rejoice as we read this wonderful New Covenant word. God promises never to remove His lovingkindness from us, no matter how badly we may fall. Yet many believers skip lightly over the heavy warning in this passage: If we forsake God's Law and refuse to keep His commands, He will visit our transgressions with His divine rod.

There simply is not any way to soften this difficult word. God is telling us plainly, in clear, New Covenant language, "If you continue in sin, I am going to deal with it severely. I will pardon you and forgive you, but I am going to take vengeance on your sin. You are going to feel My stripes on your back."

The Bible tells us that whomever the Lord loves, He chastens. We see this truth vividly illustrated in the life of David. Consider how God dealt with this man, a faithful servant who enjoyed the Lord's favor. At one point in his life, David sinned awfully, covering it up, justifying it and keeping it hidden for months on end. Finally, however, God said, "Enough"—and He sent a prophet to expose David's sin. Nathan used an analogy to tear apart every excuse David had, until finally the king admitted, "Yes, I've sinned. I'm the guilty man."

Simply admitting sin is not enough, however. God not only exposed David but He laid His divine rod across His servant's back. Of course, we know the Lord always applies His rod in love, but David's life clearly shows us that feeling God's rod of correction is no light thing. The stripes it causes are agonizing and can last a lifetime in consequences. Often the rod falls not only on us but also on our loved ones and those near us.

Consider the direct results of David's sin on those around him: The illegitimate baby he sired with Bathsheba died. Thousands of Israelite soldiers were killed in battle. He brought scandal to his country, making Israel a laughingstock in the eyes of her enemies. And in addition to all that agony, David endured endless personal pain because of his sin by losing the throne of Israel to his rebellious son, Absalom. He was hunted down like a wild animal by Absalom's army and had to flee into the wilderness from the son he loved so much. He wept uncontrollably when Absalom was killed.

Every painful event David experienced was an agonizing reminder of the consequences of his sin. He expressed his unending pain in the Psalms, writing that his soul was in constant torment, that he was cast down in confusion, that his couch was a bed of tears. He cried out, "God, why have You forsaken me?" And he wept in fear, "Holy Spirit, don't depart from me."

The implantation of godly fear by the Holy Spirit is designed to produce obedience through surrender, rather than through discipline.

4. If we continue in sin, we will experience a constant drain of peace and strength.

David wrote, "My strength fails because of my iniquity, and my bones waste away" (Psalm 31:10). Like a hole in the oil tank of a car, your sin will slowly drain you of all your resources. Your peace, joy and strength will literally drip away until they are gone completely.

David confessed, "Nor [is there] any health in my bones because of my sin" (Psalm 38:3). He was saying, "All my strength is gone because of my sin. My body has become weak and weary because of what I have done. My iniquity simply won't allow me to rest."

David was experiencing God's piercing arrows. He wrote, "Your arrows pierce me deeply, and Your hand presses me down" (Psalm 38:2). This beloved servant was being taught the fear of God and part of his painful lesson was that he had lost the peace of the Lord. Now he cried out, "He weakened my strength" (Psalm 102:23).

I know Christians who lead lives of utter confusion because they continue to indulge in sin. These hollow souls are always downcast, weak, forever struggling but getting nowhere. I also know ministers who cannot sit still because of their sin. They are constantly busy, ever moving, never entering into the Lord's rest.

It does not matter who you are—if you harbor a secret sin, you will experience continual disturbances in your life, your home, your family, your work. Everything you touch will be out of kilter. You will become increasingly restless, confused, tossed about by endless worries and fears. All your peace and strength will be drained from you.

New Covenant fear of God is heaven's antidote for casualness toward once-besetting sins. This Holy Spirit–given fear is the open door to supernatural peace and strength. The precious fear of God prepares the heart to receive every other covenant blessing.

> *5. One of the most grievous consequences of continuing in sin is the loss of usefulness to God's Kingdom.*

I have seen men who once were mightily used of the Spirit later be put on the shelf by God. The Lord told them, "I'm sorry, son. I love you, I forgive you, and My mercy will come through for you—but I cannot use you."

To me, this is one of the most dreadful things that could ever happen. It is what happened to Saul, the king of Israel. The Bible tells us:

> Samuel said to Saul, "You have done foolishly. You have not kept the commandment of the LORD your God, which He commanded you. For now the LORD would have established your kingdom over Israel forever. But now your kingdom shall not continue."
>
> 1 Samuel 13:13–14

What sad words. God told the king, "Saul, you could have had My blessing in your life continually. I was on the verge of establishing your kingdom in Israel forever. I had great plans for you, plans to use you mightily, but you would not deal with your sin. Instead, you became even more bitter and hard-hearted. So, now, I am through with you."

Immediately, God's Spirit left the king—and in that moment, Saul was no longer of use to the kingdom. Scripture reveals that from that point forward, everything Saul did was in the flesh. He ended up confiding in a witch just hours before his death.

That is where it all ends when you continue in sin: You become barren and fruitless.

FROM CONVICTION TO COMFORT

The Word declares that the fear of God is a fountain of life (see Proverbs 14:27). Also, this fear helps one to avoid the snares of death. In Proverbs 3:7 we read, "Fear the LORD and depart from evil," and in Hebrews 12:28 we are instructed to "serve God acceptably with reverence and godly fear." Those who desire to walk in the fear of God will soon be led into the full revelation of the promises and provisions of the New Covenant.

Perhaps God is dealing with you about your sin right now. He has shot His arrows of conviction into your heart, and you are feeling a sense of guilt over your sin. Do not panic—that is the gift of God. He is planting His divine power in you, teaching you, "Only through My holy fear will you depart from your sin."

Once you are convinced of the exceeding sinfulness of your actions, you will be ready for the comfort of the Holy Spirit. The book of Acts tells us, "Then the churches throughout all Judea, Galilee, and Samaria had peace and were edified. And walking in the fear of the Lord and in the comfort of the Holy Spirit, they were multiplied" (Acts 9:31). Do you see the writer's point here? As these first-century Christians walked in the fear of God, they received the comfort of the Holy Spirit.

What exactly does it mean to walk in the fear of the Lord? In short, it means reminding yourself of His warnings. Also, it means allowing the Holy Spirit to bring your sins out into the open for you to acknowledge and cast them far away from you. In doing this, He is laying the foundation to fulfill every one of God's covenant promises to you.

Then, when the fear of God has fully laid hold of you, you will dread the danger and consequences of sin. You will have the power of godly fear at work in you, and you will walk every day in this holy fear. Finally, you will see that all along God has been mercifully at work in you, doing what He promised—delivering you from the dominion and slavery of sin. The Old Covenant has finished its work—and now you can trust God to bring you into all the provisions and blessings of the New.

DISCUSSION QUESTIONS

1. God has to accomplish a certain work in us before we can lay claim to any covenant promise. What is this significant work? What is the scriptural basis for this? (Page 91)

2. How does the Holy Spirit change the way we look at sin? (Page 92)

3. List the five things God uses to create an understanding of the dangers and consequences of sin. Then list a supporting Scripture passage for each. (Pages 94–100)

4. What is one of the most grievous consequences of continuing in sin? (Page 100)

5. Read Acts 9:31. If we are convicted by the Holy Spirit and walk in the fear of the Lord, what can we expect Him to give us? (Page 102)

6. What does it mean to walk in the fear of the Lord? (Page 102)

7

THE DELIVERING POWER
OF THE NEW COVENANT

Now it happened in the process of time that the king of Egypt died. Then the children of Israel groaned because of the bondage, and they cried out; and their cry came up to God because of the bondage. So God heard their groaning, and *God remembered His covenant with Abraham, with Isaac, and with Jacob.* And God looked upon the children of Israel, and God acknowledged them.

Exodus 2:23–25, emphasis added

The king of Egypt in this passage was the ruler from whom Moses had fled many years before. Now that king was dead, and a new monarch had risen—one even more vile and contemptuous of Israel. This new king imposed stricter bondage and worse hardships on the Israelites. Not only did they have to produce a higher quota of bricks, but they had to gather their own straw to bind them. When they failed to find enough straw to keep the bricks from crumbling, the Egyptians' whips came down on their backs harder than ever.

Soon the Israelites were driven to despair. The women and children were forced into slave labor, having to roam the dry countryside to gather whatever straw they could find. Every day in the fields they were beaten, and every night they limped home, collapsing under the bondage. They were wounded, oppressed and depressed.

Finally, their cries of agony and hopelessness reached high into the heavens, and God responded: "Israel groaned because of the bondage, and they cried out; and their cry came up to God because of the bondage. So God heard their groaning" (Exodus 2:23–24).

Bear in mind, the nation of Israel had labored in slavery for many years, weeping and sorrowing over their endless bondage. Yet here, the phrase "God heard" suggests the Lord was suddenly moved to action. Why did God wait until now to move on their behalf?

At this point, Scripture tells us that God remembered His covenant with them (see verse 24). The Hebrew wording here is, "God took notice of them." Does this mean the Lord had forgotten His people all those previous years, ignoring their pleas? Does it mean He had suffered a lapse of memory but now, suddenly, He remembered His covenant to protect, deliver and shield Abraham's seed?

No, of course not. In fact, Israel still received the blessings of God's Abrahamic covenant even while in bondage. They multiplied in population, just as the Lord had promised. It did not matter that they were enslaved; God still honored His word to them, blessing not only Abraham, Isaac and Jacob, but all their seed who followed. "I will establish My covenant between Me and you and your descendants after you in their generations, for an everlasting covenant, to be God to you and your descendants after you" (Genesis 17:7).

WHAT WENT WRONG?

The important question is, How could Israel live for so many years in such bondage and hopelessness, when God had given her an everlasting promise to shield and preserve her? He had never annulled His covenant with the Israelites; it was theirs to be claimed the whole time. So why did they ignore it all those years? Why did they never appeal to Him regarding the covenant, laying hold of God's incredible promises?

You might think, "The answer is obvious. The Lord clearly forewarned Abraham that Israel would be in bondage for a time." Indeed, God's Word says:

> "Know certainly that your descendants will be strangers in a land that is not theirs, and will serve them, and they will afflict them four hundred years. . . . But in the fourth generation they shall return here, for the iniquity of the Amorites is not yet complete."
>
> Genesis 15:13, 16

The Lord *predicted* enslavement of the Israelites, yet their affliction was not *foreordained*. God was simply speaking here by foreknowledge. He knew their idolatry in Egypt would bring on their great affliction. He did not suspend His covenant blessings toward Israel until the heathen nation's "cup of iniquity" was filled. And He did not send the Israelites to Egypt as a kind of chastisement. On the contrary, His Word says He sent Jacob to Egypt in order to "preserve a posterity for [Israel] in the earth, and to save your lives by a great deliverance" (Genesis 45:7).

God never intended the Israelites to become slaves; He was simply forecasting the slavery that sin would bring upon them. His plan was for Israel to become a mighty nation shielded from idolatry and preserved as a people of God.

So, how did the Israelites forget this covenant? Simply put, they were blinded to it by sin. Somehow, they fell into lustful, sensual idolatry. In the New Testament, Stephen quotes God's words to His people given through the Old Testament prophet Amos: "You also took up the tabernacle of Moloch, and the star of your god Remphan, images which you made to worship; and I will carry you away beyond Babylon" (Acts 7:43).

The enslaved Israelites did not remember anything about God's covenant. They cried and sighed for years, suffering great agony, never once laying hold of His promises. They knew, of course, all about God's dealings with their father, Abraham, and they knew that Jacob had laid hold of the covenant on many occasions. They knew he was delivered from his brother, Esau, by God's covenant, and they knew he was instructed to go to Egypt because of the covenant. They also knew that Jacob's son Joseph went to Egypt by covenant in order to work out a mighty deliverance for Israel, not slavery.

These patriarchs never forgot the covenant God had made with them. Its truth had been opened to them, and they simply believed it and claimed it. Over time, however, the nation of Israel forgot the wonderful message of God's covenant. The people neglected it, turning instead to self-gratification. They sought only to please their flesh, never removing the idolatry from their hearts. So they remained enslaved, without victory— even though the covenant was still theirs to be claimed.

Abraham was to do two things as his part of the covenant. First, he was to walk blamelessly before the Lord. And, second, he was to trust almighty God to be his shield, protector and great reward. Abraham was faithful to do both of these things. Yet now, as God looked upon His servant's seed, He saw a sin-saturated people—spiritually blind and unable to deliver themselves, sinking ever deeper in despair. They had lost hope because they had not kept their part of the pledge. They had forgotten the covenant.

But God had not. He said, "I am going to rise up now and keep My promise. Though Abraham's children have forgotten My word to them, I will never forget it. I am going to deliver them."

When the Lord saw His people's oppression and heard their cry for help, He moved in to fulfill His terms of the covenant. "I have come down to deliver them out of the hand of the Egyptians, and to bring them up from that land to a good and large land" (Exodus 3:8). God took the matter completely out of Israel's hands and placed it in His own. His people were powerless, without the strength or ability to deliver themselves. Their salvation had to come by His grace and mercy alone—through covenant. This is the one truth we must fully grasp if we are to understand the purpose of the New Covenant. God swears by oath that He will take matters into His own hands and by His power alone deliver us from all dominion of sin.

Please note that God did not deliver the Israelites because they were good people. He did it for the sole reason that He had made a covenant with Abraham. Israel never would have been delivered if God had not acted in covenant agreement.

Moreover, the Lord already had deliverance planned for His people. He had a man prepared, one who would bring His people out of Egypt (see Exodus 3:10). Moses was God's deliverer for His people at that time, to move them out of the bondage of sin.

LIVING IN BONDAGE TODAY

This brings us to the present generation. Today God's people are once again living in a time of bondage. They are enslaved by lust, living under the dominion of sin, and I believe their sighs and groans are reaching heaven. Now, God is once more unveiling His New Covenant.

In Egypt, the cries God heard came from fewer than three million people. His followers were located in a relatively small parcel of territory called Goshen. Today, the same cries go up worldwide from the hearts of multiplied millions of God's people. Like the Israelites in Egypt, these believers continue in slavery year after year, bound and driven by their sin. It has become their daily taskmaster, lashing them with such torment they are ready to collapse. They cry out daily, "Oh, Lord, will I never be free? What do I have to do to be delivered from these chains? I've prayed, I've fasted, I've pored over the Scriptures, but I still can't get victory. Where is the power that will deliver me from this bondage?"

Many people eventually resign themselves to their sins as if they are cursed to a lifelong battle they will never win. In despair, many give themselves over to their lusts completely, convinced that they tried but God failed them. They reason, "Everybody told me the power of the Holy Spirit would be available to me. But I never experienced it."

Beloved, God foresaw the wicked days we are living in. In His great omniscience, He knew the overwhelming sinfulness and the great falling away that would strike His people in these last days. And He determined all along to bring us deliverance.

GOD'S UNTRUSTWORTHY PARTNER

In this covenant, God pledges to do the following four things:

1. He swears to write His law on our hearts and minds.

2. He takes an oath that He will be God to us, and that we will be His children.

I still pray, read God's Word and do good deeds, but the reason I do them has totally changed.

I accepted Jesus into my heart in 1990 at age 39. I was on Rikers Island at the time and had spent a lot of my life in prison. One would think that after accepting Jesus, my cycle of drugs and crime would stop, but I was bound. Prison became like a revolving door for me.

Even though I loved God and wanted desperately to please Him, I was going about it all wrong. I thought that I had to pray, read the Bible and do good deeds in order to maintain my salvation, and of course I failed constantly. Finally, in 2008, I began to get a glimpse of God's New Covenant promise. I was in prison once again and was seeking God earnestly, fasting and praying for truth. God was with me and heard my cry. He led me to Times Square Church, where I learned about the New Covenant.

This hit home with me. I realized that God had been working His New Covenant into my life during the four years I had recently spent in prison. I finally understood that I could not do anything in myself to maintain my salvation or keep myself from falling—it was all a matter of trusting in Him and His work in me.

Pastor David explained: "It is simply impossible for any believer to deliver himself from sin's dominion." First, God has to cause the sin-bound person to want to be free. And, second, God has to cause the sin-bound person to see the utter futility of his efforts to set himself free.

I needed to know that truth so badly! I had tried everything in my power to snap sin's hold on my life. It was hard for me to see that God would actually do the work. All He wanted me to do was trust Him to do it. What a wonderful, life-giving truth!

Today I still do all the things that I used to do to try to maintain my Christianity: pray, read the Word of God and do good deeds. The reason I do them has totally changed, however; now I do them simply because I love God. I am not trying to win His favor.

For the past year I have been working at Times Square Church, where I have learned to trust God in every situation. In return, God has blessed me with freedom from the bondage of sin, and He has shown me what true abundant life really is. Praise God!

—*Joseph*

3. He promises we will know Him and His ways because we will be taught by the Holy Spirit.

4. He pledges to be merciful to our unrighteousness, forgiving all our sins and iniquities.

Now, for any covenant to be made, both parties have to be trustworthy. They must be dependable, able to fulfill the agreements made between them. And they have to have the resources available to keep their promises.

The problem with humankind as a party in covenant with God is that we are neither trustworthy nor dependable. That is why God cut the covenant with His own Son. We are in no position to keep our end of any kind of agreement. Like Israel, we may say, "Yes, Lord. We'll obey everything You command us. Whatever You say, we'll gladly do." This is exactly what the Israelites said when they received the Law, but they broke the covenant within days. And today, we are no different. We are just as bankrupt as the children of Israel were. Our promises to God in a covenant, therefore, are worthless.

So, how could God ever make a covenant with us? As we have learned, we are in covenant with Him because we are in Christ and for that reason alone. Christ our mediator is worthy and dependable, and He has all the resources needed to keep our side of the covenant. We have been brought into the New Covenant with God by having faith in Jesus.

You may say, "But God still demands perfect obedience on our part. We are supposed to have total dependence on the Father, but we are imperfect beings. We simply are not able to keep the terms of His covenant." True—but the New Covenant is based on better promises, because those promises are Jesus', not ours.

Let me illustrate briefly. Let's say I wanted to sell my house. I would not even consider signing a contract with a person who was penniless, no matter how upstanding his character was or how many promises he made to pay me. I would have no choice but to tell him, "You need to find a co-signer, someone who has enough money to pay my price and make good on the deal. This person can't be somebody who has 'all but a few thousand dollars.' He has to have the whole amount in the bank, ready to hand it to me when the deal is closed."

Here's another example. Suppose you owe a million-dollar debt, and you will go to jail for life if you do not pay it. You decide to go to your local bank and meet with the loan officer. You ask him, "Sir, do you make million-dollar loans?" He answers in the affirmative. You tell him, "Great! I need a million dollars, right away."

He promptly pulls out a loan application and says, "Okay, let's list all your assets and collateral, as well as your annual income. Tell me: How do you plan to pay back the loan?"

You answer, "Well, to be honest, I'm broke. I have no assets. But I always keep my word. Just ask my family. I'll do everything that's in me to pay it back. I'll work my fingers to the bone. I'll even work nights here at the bank. I'll scrub the floors, wash the windows, do all kinds of jobs. And I'll pray in whatever I can't make. I'll also behave well the whole time I have the loan. I won't smoke, drink, lust or steal."

What do you think your chances would be of getting a loan from that banker? They would be about as good as your chances today of keeping your promises to almighty God.

Remember: The whole purpose of the Old Covenant was to show us how bankrupt and helpless we are, as well as how undependable our promises are. Today God lets us operate under the Old Covenant of works until we learn once and for all that our striving in the flesh is to no avail. Try as we might, we will eventually run out of effort, sweat until there is not a drop left and see every promise of ours fail.

The Old Covenant has completed its work when we come to the place where we finally renounce all confidence in our human strength. At that point, we say, "I can't do it. I'm dead, empty, dry, and my word is no good. I've made a million sincere promises to the Lord, but I have broken every one of them."

We then realize we need a wealthy, worthy co-signer—someone who has the resources to step in and settle our debt when we have no other way to pay it.

God's Incomprehensible Mercy

God the Father gave His Son, Jesus, access to all of His own riches and wealth. In other words, He invested in Him all the wisdom, knowledge, power and glory of heaven. And by being made wealthy in all these things, Jesus became the only one worthy to be co-signer of the covenant. "By so much more Jesus has become a surety [guarantor, sponsor, co-signer] of a better covenant" (Hebrews 7:22):

Could there be any greater mercy than this? God so loved us that He made His Son rich beyond all comprehension. Then He made Him both our kinsman and our co-signer. He has become the person responsible to settle all our debts. He pays when we cannot.

Now, whenever we run out of resources and all our debts come due, the heavenly Father in His perfect justice has every right to call for payment. But that is when our co-signer is notified, and He responds, "I'll pay it all." He does pay—He has paid—and He will pay.

Yet God's mercy is even more incomprehensible than this. When our co-signer left this earth, He ascended to the Father, taking with Him all His wealth. Right now He is in glory, while we remain here in our weakness and poverty. But the New Covenant contains a special provision to meet our need. It is this: The same Holy Spirit who empowered Christ to live a sinless life has been sent to abide in our hearts. That is correct—God's very own Spirit is our full-time, live-in attorney, acting continually on our behalf. He abides in us just as He did in Jesus.

Here is God's covenant promise regarding the Spirit:

"As for Me," says the LORD, "this is My covenant with them: My Spirit who is upon you, and My words which I have put in your mouth, shall not depart from your mouth, nor from the mouth of your descendants, nor from the mouth of your descendants' descendants," says the LORD, "from this time and forevermore."

Isaiah 59:21

Jesus sent the Holy Spirit to fill His place here on earth, and the Spirit does so in the following ways:

1. He guides us into all truth, speaking whatever Christ tells Him to speak.

2. He shows us things to come. These things have to do with all the resources we have in Christ's riches in glory—the keeping power, wisdom, might and glory of God.

3. He glorifies Christ. How? He shows us all the riches that are available to us in Jesus. "He will glorify Me, for He will take of what is Mine and declare it to you" (John 16:14).

4. He delivers to us all that the Father has given His Son. "All things that the Father has are Mine. Therefore I said that He will take of Mine and declare it to you" (verse 15).

Jesus is saying, "God has made Me rich on your account. He is taking what He has given to Me and is giving it to you."

Accessing Our Resources

The Holy Spirit is the Lawgiver—whose very finger wrote the commandments on stone. Today the same Spirit writes God's Law in our hearts. He shows us the will of the Father and the mind of Christ.

The Spirit also distributes to us all the power, strength and riches of Christ we need to overcome sin. He is the One we are to depend on to defeat Satan and rob him of his power against us. "If by the Spirit you put to death the deeds of the body, you will live" (Romans 8:13).

God tells us, "I am going to come to you in your struggles, just as I came to the Israelites in Egypt when they groaned and cried. I sent them a deliverer in Moses—and now I have sent you a deliverer in My Son, Jesus. His Spirit lives forever in your hearts as your attorney. So, whenever you run out of resources and are about to fall, just notify your co-signer. Tell Him what you need and He will provide all the wisdom, strength, power and help necessary."

Have you accepted this incredible truth? Do you believe that Jesus agreed in covenant to keep you from falling, guaranteeing you would never be forsaken, and you would be able to obey Him fully and live in victory? Believe it—because He guaranteed it on His own worthy name. You were not the one who made a worthy oath, who provided a co-signer, who found an attorney. God did all of this for you, and now He wants to use it all to redeem you fully from the dominion of sin.

How to Take Part

How can this promise of a new heart hold true for a people who have no desire to know the Lord in fullness? Why would He waste His mercy on those who have no intention of departing from their sins?

Today, God is once again remembering His covenant with His people in their time of great bondage. He has heard the sighing and crying of a people who hunger for freedom. And He is saying to us, "You have lost the truth of the covenant. And now, unless I reveal again My covenant, you have no hope." His Word commands us, "Hold fast My covenant. . . . I will give them an everlasting name that shall not be cut off . . . [everyone who] holds fast My covenant" (Isaiah 56:4–6).

I am convinced that the revelation of God's New Covenant will be the one message in these last days that sets people free from sin's dominion. Yes, wickedness is going to abound more than the world has ever seen, but God will bring forth the truth of His New Covenant to free His people. He knows only it can stand against the onslaught of a mad devil.

We may have forgotten this truth over the years, but our Lord has not—and He never will. Right now, He is looking upon us as He looked upon Israel in Egypt, and once again He is coming to deliver His people through covenant.

DISCUSSION QUESTIONS

1. When the Israelites were taken into slavery in Egypt, they forgot God's covenant promise to them. How could this have happened? (Page 108)

2. What are the two things Abraham was to do as his part of the covenant? (Page 108)

3. Read Exodus 3:8. When God saw Israel's oppression and heard her cry for help, what was His response? (Page 109)

4. What is the one truth we must grasp if we are to understand the purpose of the New Covenant? (Page 109)

5. What are the four things God pledges to do in the New Covenant? (Pages 110, 112)

6. The Old Covenant has completed its work when what happens? (Page 114)

7. Name four ways the Holy Spirit fills or takes Jesus' place here on earth. (Page 116)

8. What does God mean when He says that He covenants to write His laws in our hearts and that we would learn of Him? (Page 117)

8

CHRIST, OUR HIGH PRIEST
OF THE NEW COVENANT

Let me tell you the story of a boy king who came to Judah's throne at age sixteen. His name was Uzziah, which in Hebrew means "strength with God." This king was a seeker after God from his early years, and Scripture tells us, "As long as he sought the LORD, God made him prosper" (2 Chronicles 26:5).

Uzziah's mother was named Jecholiah, meaning "God will enable." Evidently, Jecholiah was a godly woman who taught her son God's ways. It is possible that she gave her son the name Uzziah because she wanted him to have the strength of the Lord throughout his life, for God's holy purposes.

Another powerful influence in Uzziah's life was the prophet Zechariah, a contemporary of the prophet Isaiah. Scripture says this righteous man "had understanding in the visions of God" (verse 5). Zechariah was a pious man of God who served the

Lord faithfully as long as he lived. He also taught Uzziah the ways of the Lord.

The Bible makes a simple but profound statement about Uzziah. It says, "God helped him" (verse 7). God prospered this young man mightily. Uzziah became one of the most powerful, successful kings of his day, reigning over Judah for 52 years (see verse 3). Throughout those years, Scripture says, he continued to seek the Lord. Indeed, we may gather that Uzziah's strength was not just military and material, but moral as well. We read that he wiped out all idolatry from the land, and this bold action only added to his fame. There was something obviously different about Uzziah. He had strong character—and this was because God's Word had been imbedded in his heart from his early years. His caring mother and the godly prophet Zechariah had seen to that.

Yet, after five decades of walking faithfully before the Lord and calling on God's name, Uzziah made a tragic mistake. At the peak of his strength, Uzziah transgressed against the Lord: "But when he was strong his heart was lifted up, to his destruction, for he transgressed against the LORD his God by entering the temple of the LORD to burn incense on the altar of incense" (verse 16).

Uzziah committed a horrible sin: He attempted to make himself the high priest of Judah. In just a few short verses, Scripture describes this outlandish act by the king. First, he made himself a brazen censer and filled it with fire of his own making—"strange fire"—rather than with the consecrated fire of the incense altar. Then Uzziah proceeded to march into the holy place, to function as a priest.

He never made it. Azariah, the high priest, and eighty other priests blocked his way. They told him in no uncertain terms, "It is not for you, Uzziah, to burn incense to the LORD, but for the priests, the sons of Aaron, who are consecrated to burn incense" (verse 18). They said, "Uzziah, you're not appointed to do this. You know better. You're not from the priestly lineage God Himself has ordained. This is a wicked thing you are trying to do. You're simply not called to do it."

When Uzziah heard this, he raged at the priests. Then something frightening happened: "Then Uzziah became furious. . . . And while he was angry with the priests, leprosy broke out on his forehead, before the priests in the house of the LORD, beside the incense altar" (verse 19). Before Uzziah could take another step, leprosy broke out on his forehead.

Suddenly the errant king recognized what was happening, and before he could further desecrate the Temple the priests drove him out: "They thrust him out of that place. Indeed he also hurried to get out, because the LORD had struck him" (verse 20). The disgraced king raced out of the Temple.

A WARNING FOR THE RIGHTEOUS

You may be wondering, "What does this story have to do with us today? What does it have to do with the covenant? I know Paul says that everything recorded in the Old Testament is meant for our instruction and understanding, but I just don't get the lesson here."

Is this story meant to teach us how it is possible to fail God after years of following Him, if we suddenly grow proud of our own strength? Yes, it is about that—but it is also about much more. Is it about discerning the dangers and pitfalls of success and prosperity? Yes, it is about that, too—but, again, this story is about much more.

This passage is about the sin of the very religious. It is meant for believers who have walked with the Lord faithfully over a long period—people who have gained great moral strength and have been blessed by God as a result. Like Uzziah, they are neither immoral nor unfaithful, always striving to do what is right in God's eyes. And because of their upright lives, whenever they hear a message on sin, they are able to say to themselves genuinely: "I'm so glad that message doesn't apply to me. I'm not under the dominion of any particular sin. I know of no bondage, lust, habit or bitterness in my life. I can honestly say with Paul, 'I have fought a good fight.'"

We all know these kinds of believers. They truly are a blessing to be around. Yet King Uzziah was this very same kind of servant of the Lord—and the Bible clearly tells us his fifty years of faithful service to God ended in vain. How could such a morally strong man end up transgressing the Lord's commandments? How could someone so helped by God for so many years end up under judgment, an ostracized leper?

I believe Uzziah's story is meant as a warning to every righteous believer living today. Think about it. Uzziah lived a clean, moral life. He sat under the ministry of two powerful prophets, Zechariah and Isaiah, and ruled righteously for fifty years. So, what was so awful about what he did in the Temple that God should disregard all those years of goodness? How could fifty years of moral strength end up as filthy rags in the eyes of the Lord?

Why Was God So Angry?

Uzziah drew God's wrath by attempting to act as his own high priest. His reasoning was something like this: "I'm as holy as any priest. I've spent fifty years seeking the Lord. I am morally clean and spiritually strong in my walk with God. There isn't any evil in me. Surely all my good works over the years have built up a reserve account for me with God. So, I'll just go directly into the holy place and present my fifty years of faithfulness to Him as a sacrifice. That should be wholly acceptable to Him."

There is great danger in trying to come into the presence of a holy God—into the holy of holies—with our own strange fire, our own censer of good works. You might think, "I already know that. I am not like Uzziah. I realize Jesus Christ is my only High Priest. I wouldn't ever think of trying to present my own sacrifice to the Lord. I wouldn't dare go into His presence thinking my righteousness or good works have any merit whatsoever. Whatever transgression Uzziah committed, I am not guilty of it."

Yet many honest, righteous believers do indeed set themselves up as their own high priests. They enter into the holy of holies with strange fire, just as Uzziah did. They carry into God's presence a censer of their own goodness, energy, abilities and will. They claim the high priesthood for themselves—and, whether they realize it or not, they bypass the high priesthood of Christ.

Do not think this never happens among dedicated followers of Jesus. You see, there comes a time in every believer's life—usually when it is least expected—when the enemy comes in like a flood with overwhelming temptations, resurgent lusts, unanticipated failures. This is the time when a Christian is most tempted to act as his own high priest. A moment comes when he has to decide whether he will try to sacrifice on his own behalf, or rely on the high priesthood of Jesus Christ to deliver him.

THE HIGH PRIESTHOOD OF CHRIST

The first seven chapters of Hebrews are full of lessons on faith, holiness, hearing God's voice, divine rest, prayer, covenants, the

125

ministry of the Holy Spirit and much more. Then, in chapter 8, the author states, "Now this is the main point of the things we are saying" (Hebrews 8:1). He is telling us, "Here is the point. Everything I have laid out to you in the previous seven chapters is summed up in this one concept. So, if you don't get it here, you have missed it all."

Now comes the point of it all—the highest thing we could understand: "We have such a High Priest, who is seated at the right hand of the throne of the Majesty in the heavens" (Hebrews 8:1). The keystone of all Gospel preaching and spiritual understanding is this: We have a High Priest on the throne in glory. Jesus Christ is our merciful, compassionate Redeemer who stands in the very presence of the Father and intercedes for us. He wants us to know that the battle is no longer ours, because He is doing all the work of intercession for us. And He is doing it in keeping with the covenant He made with the Father in eternity.

Let me explain a bit more about the high priesthood of Christ. In ancient Israel, when the high priest entered the holy of holies, he did not go in without taking blood. Once he was inside the inner sanctum, he made atonement for the sins of the people: "Into the second part [of the Tabernacle] the high priest went alone once a year, not without blood, which he offered for himself and for the people's sins committed in ignorance" (Hebrews 9:7).

Here is the difference today under the New Covenant, with Christ in the role of our High Priest: "Not with the blood of goats and calves, but with His own blood [Christ] entered the Most Holy Place once for all, having obtained eternal redemption" (Hebrews 9:12). "For Christ has not entered the holy places made with hands, which are copies of the true, but into heaven itself, now to appear in the presence of God for us" (Hebrews

9:24). "For by one offering He has perfected forever those who are being sanctified" (Hebrews 10:14).

Over and over we see the author's point: Christ is our one and only High Priest, and His one sacrifice suffices for all our needs, for all time. To drive home the point, the author quotes the prophet Jeremiah:

> "This is the covenant that I will make with them after those days, says the Lord: I will put My laws into their hearts, and in their minds I will write them," then He adds, "Their sins and their lawless deeds [iniquities] I will remember no more." Now where there is remission of these, there is no longer an offering for sin. Therefore, brethren, having boldness to enter the Holiest by the blood of Jesus, by a new and living way which He consecrated for us, through the veil, that is, His flesh, and having a High Priest over the house of God, let us draw near with a true heart in full assurance of faith, having our hearts sprinkled from an evil conscience and our bodies washed with pure water.
>
> Hebrews 10:16–22

We learn here that our High Priest instituted a New Covenant, or agreement, in which He says He will write His laws in our hearts. Moreover, He promises to teach us His ways and keep us in His holiness. His agent to do this is the Holy Spirit. After the author outlines all these wonderful truths, he gives a powerful warning. In so many words, this warning is the same one given to Uzziah:

> If we sin willfully after we have received the knowledge of the truth, there no longer remains a sacrifice for sins, but a certain fearful expectation of judgment, and fiery indignation which will devour the adversaries. Anyone who has rejected Moses' law dies without mercy on the testimony of two or three witnesses. Of how much worse punishment, do you suppose, will he be

thought worthy who has trampled the Son of God underfoot, counted the blood of the covenant by which he was sanctified a common thing, and insulted the Spirit of grace? For we know Him who said, "Vengeance is Mine, I will repay," says the Lord. And again, "The Lord will judge His people."

Hebrews 10:26–30

The author of this passage is giving us a sober warning: "You have freely received the knowledge of Christ's high priesthood. Now, if you don't rest on His blood sacrifice—if you attempt to be your own high priest, resisting sin in your own power and bringing to God the strange fire of your own human energy—your offering will be unacceptable. There is no sacrifice other than Christ's. If you bypass His sacrifice in favor of your own, you count unworthy the blood of His covenant. You insult Christ, your one and only High Priest—and you will suffer His vengeance."

Uzziah tried to come into God's presence without blood— that is, bringing his own sacrifice, energy and good works. Yet there is no other way to the Father but through the covenant blood—Christ's own blood.

Perhaps you are able to say, "Thank God—I'm a long-standing, faithful, pure servant of the Lord." If this is so, I do not belittle your moral goodness. I thank God for every saint who has a testimony to the overcoming work of the Holy Spirit. Rather, I am speaking to the good person who tries to enter God's presence as his own high priest. Such a person comes to God's altar carrying a censer filled with strange fire—trying to plead his own case, making intercession for himself, telling God how hard he has worked to do right.

I know a pastor in his early sixties who has served God faithfully for all his years. Since the day he met the Lord, he lived free of any plaguing evil thoughts. But suddenly, in his later years,

The harder we try to please, the more imprisoned we become.

My husband and I were brought up in a legalistic religion and were heavily indoctrinated in the tradition of works as a way of walking in holiness.

I would lie awake at night crying out to God for help, knowing that somewhere, somehow there was more to life than we were experiencing. The rules of our church and the demands of our leaders were senseless to us. For instance, if our clothing did not meet certain standards, we would be asked to make a public confession and change them or be excommunicated—which meant certain damnation.

There was no life, no assurance of salvation—no hope! We were not allowed to "know that you are saved," which was confusing. As we searched the Scriptures, what we found written there did not line up with what we were being taught, but we didn't know how to sort it out. This led to feelings of hopelessness and depression.

Through a wonderful set of circumstances we found ourselves at a tent revival in our community. Attending such an event was absolutely against the rules of our church, but it was there we found the answers we had been seeking. Forever engraved in my mind is the picture of the pastor praying with the worship band at the beginning of the service. (All our lives we had been taught that musical instruments are sinful.) He opened the Word of God and read Psalm 150, where God clearly instructs us to praise Him with a trumpet, a lute and a harp, with tambourines and dancing, with strings and flutes, and with a loud clash of cymbals. We are to praise the Lord!

Instantly I knew that we had been walking in error all our lives. God opened our ears and hearts to hear what the Holy Spirit was saying, and in the years to follow we found that the devil could no longer oppress us.

God promises to remember His covenant with His people in their time of great bondage. He hears the cry of a people who hunger for freedom. Jesus paid the price for our sins, and we are free!

—*Linda*

he was struck down with a deep, horrible depression. A dark cloud came upon him from out of nowhere—and in the pit of his depression, evil thoughts of lust began to plague his mind.

This man could not understand what was happening. He cried out, "Oh, Lord, where did this come from? What is happening to me?" But the heavens seemed closed—and the evil thoughts persisted.

Finally, the godly minister saw that he had two options. First, he could cast himself to the ground—weeping, mourning and wallowing in despair over a sin he could not comprehend. He could allow fear to overcome him and the devil to fill him with dread. He could turn inward, feeling unworthy, lost, wicked. And he could act as his own high priest, trying everything in his own power to straighten out what had happened. He could pray, "Lord, You know this isn't like me. If You will just give me time and be patient with me, I will get on top of it. I will do my best never again to think these evil thoughts. I want to get back to where I was before this hellish invasion came upon me. Whatever it takes, I'll pull myself out of it."

But if the minister did this, he would be doing exactly as Uzziah had done. He would be entering the holy place with strange fire—his censer filled with human energy and the works of the flesh. He would be striving, working, operating under his own power to set himself free.

Thank God, this servant of the Lord chose the second option. He quickly realized, "I'm no high priest," and he turned to the one and only High Priest, Jesus Christ. He prayed, "Lord, I don't know what has happened, but You have promised me by Your covenant that You would see me through—and I believe You.

"You commanded me to bring every thought captive to obedience to Your Word, but right now You know I have no human strength to do that. All these evil thoughts are raging in my mind, and I can't stop them. Satan is plaguing me with them. Yet, Jesus, You made a covenant to put within me a new heart and a new mind. You said You would forgive me and keep me, and that Your Holy Spirit would empower me to overcome. So now, Lord, I come boldly on the grounds of Your covenant, to obtain all the power You have promised me through Your Spirit. I step out in faith in that power, trusting You to deliver me from my oppressor."

The minister then stood still and waited to see the salvation of the Lord. And, indeed, God delivered him by heavenly power—through the mercy, grace, energy and fire of the Holy Spirit.

It is not enough for us to know we have a High Priest in heaven. We have to see Him as our merciful, comforting High Priest—our intercessor in all our sufferings and temptations. No matter what we are going through, no matter what temptation we face, He has been there before us. He knows what it is like for us, and that is why we can expect mercy from Him.

Our loving High Priest never holds back His forgiveness from us. He is ready at all times to pour out on us all the grace and mercy we need. "For You, Lord, are good, and ready to forgive, and abundant in mercy to all those who call upon You" (Psalm 86:5). "The LORD is merciful and gracious, slow to anger, and abounding in mercy" (Psalm 103:8). "With the LORD there is mercy, and with Him is abundant redemption" (Psalm 130:7).

Everything our God has for us is abundant, plenteous—more than enough, more than sufficient, more than we could ever need.

INIQUITY WILL ALWAYS BREAK OUT

Now let's examine the sad end of Uzziah.

> Leprosy broke out on his forehead, before the priests in the house of the Lord, beside the incense altar. And Azariah the chief priest

and all the priests looked at him, and . . . they thrust him out of that place. Indeed he also hurried to get out, because the LORD had struck him. King Uzziah was a leper until the day of his death. He dwelt in an isolated house, because he was a leper; for he was cut off from the house of the LORD.

2 Chronicles 26:19–21

In the end, what does Uzziah's story say to us? It tells us that no matter how hard we may try to conquer sin—no matter how much we may trust in our own works, flesh and energy to get victory—the leprosy of sin will keep breaking out on us. Just when we believe we have something to give to God, when we think we are on top of our sin, more than a conqueror, our iniquity breaks out once more.

Uzziah thought he was holy because of his fifty years of faithfulness to God, but the moment he tried to act as his own high priest, he saw his true condition. Likewise today, whenever we try to bring our own works and energy to God, the Holy Spirit causes us to realize just how weak and unclean we are. We fall back into a sin we thought we had conquered and discover there is no good thing in us—no merit or righteousness at all. We see our need for a high priest to cleanse us of our leprosy.

Thank God, we have such a High Priest! He tenderly heals our leprosy, patiently forgives our sin and supernaturally restores our souls.

ISAIAH SEES OUR HIGH PRIEST

We understand in reading King Uzziah's story that the prophet Isaiah loved this man. He was his friend and counselor, so Isaiah had to be deeply grieved when he heard how Uzziah had sinned. It must have broken his heart to see his king wasting away his final days as a leper. Apparently, Uzziah spent his last few years in an infirmary.

When the king finally died, Isaiah's soul felt a tremendous impact. As he thought about all that had happened, he lifted his eyes to heaven and declared, "In the year that King Uzziah died, I saw the Lord sitting on a throne, high and lifted up, and the train of His robe filled the temple" (Isaiah 6:1). The prophet saw clearly what happens whenever someone tries to bring strange fire into the holy presence of God. His soul was so stirred at the thought, he cried, "There is only one High Priest—and He is enthroned in heaven. The Lord has allowed me to see our High Priest and it isn't King Uzziah. Our High Priest is high, holy, lifted up above all."

Isaiah was foreseeing the priesthood of Jesus Christ, in all His glory and power. He was moved to cry, "Get your eyes on the one and only High Priest! He is high and holy, and the whole earth is full of His glory."

What happens next is simply amazing. As the prophet stood before God's awesome holiness, he cried, "Woe is me, for I am undone! Because I am a man of unclean lips, and I dwell in the midst of a people of unclean lips; for my eyes have seen the King, the LORD of hosts" (Isaiah 6:5).

Lepers in that day had to cover their upper lip with a rag or cloth, signifying their uncleanness. So, when Isaiah spoke here of being "a man of unclean lips," he was talking about his own spiritual leprosy. He was saying, "King Uzziah was a leper all along, but he never knew it. And now I see I'm a leper too. We're all lepers. We are so distant from the Lord's holiness, we are utterly sin-sick." He saw the total otherness of God. There is no way to bridge that distance, to cross the chasm. It takes a miracle of grace only our Lord can provide.

So, what did Isaiah do at that point? Did he leave God's presence, as Uzziah did? Did he turn to self-effort? No—Isaiah immediately humbled himself, bowing before the holiness he saw before him.

How was the prophet cleansed? How was his iniquity purged? Did he accomplish it himself, by his own will, energy and determination? No. He simply believed—and he waited for the Spirit to do the work and, true to His word, God did it all. He sent one of the seraphim to Isaiah with a live coal in his hand who laid the coal on Isaiah's lips, purifying them by fire. The prophet was cleansed—all by the work of the One who sat on the throne.

Clearly, Isaiah was foreseeing the coming ministry of Christ. That is why he is saying to us today, "Uzziah wasn't the only leper. We are all lepers in need of cleansing, and our own fleshly works and energy won't suffice. The only energy that can help us overcome is the fire of the Holy Spirit."

This is what the New Covenant is all about. The Old Covenant was meant to show us how leprous we are and how incapable we are of healing ourselves. But now, in His New Covenant, God is saying to us, "My child, I know you cannot do it, so I am going to provide for you. I know your heart is wicked, so I am going to give you a new heart. I know you have no strength to please Me, so I am going to cause you to desire to do My good pleasure. I will take out your heart of stone and give you a heart of flesh.

"You may not understand all of this," He is saying, "but I will send you My Spirit, and He will teach you everything. When He comes to live in you, He will begin writing all My commands on your heart and mind. From then on, My Word will be with you night and day. I am going to do it all for you."

Remember—the power is always His, not ours. The Holy Spirit activates all the graces and mercies of Christ given to us when we believed in His saving power. You have a Man in glory—a God-man who retained His humanity and who still is touched by your feelings and needs. He will send you greater fillings of His Spirit to work a complete deliverance in you from all power and dominion of sin. All that is needed on your part is your step of faith.

Go to your High Priest and ask Him for a greater infusion of the Spirit to set you free.

DISCUSSION QUESTIONS

1. What was the sin of King Uzziah that so angered God? (Page 122)

2. What is the primary lesson we are to learn from the sin of King Uzziah? (Page 125)

3. What is the main point of Hebrews 8:1? (Page 126)

4. Our High Priest, Jesus Christ, instituted a New Covenant. Where will He write His laws? What does He promise to teach us? How will He accomplish this? (Page 126)

5. When we try to please God through our own striving and effort, how does God respond? Why does He respond this way? (Page 132)

6. Uzziah developed leprosy the moment he sinned in the Temple. In Scripture, what does leprosy represent? (Page 132)

7. When Isaiah was so strongly impacted by his vision of God high and lifted up, how did he react? (Page 133)

8. When Isaiah spoke of being "a man of unclean lips," what was he talking about? (Page 133)

9. The Old Covenant was meant to show us how "leprous" we are. What does the New Covenant show us? (Page 134)

9

THE NEW COVENANT DESTROYS SATANIC STRONGHOLDS

The seventh chapter of Micah contains one of the most powerful messages on the New Covenant ever preached. In this incredible sermon, Micah is speaking to natural Israel, yet he is also speaking to the Church of Jesus Christ in these last days. He begins his sermon with a heartbroken cry—one that is still being heard from spiritually starved believers around the world today: "Woe is me! . . . There is no cluster to eat" (Micah 7:1).

Micah is describing the effect of a famine in Israel—a famine of food and of God's Word. It echoes the words of an earlier prophecy by Amos:

"Behold, the days are coming," says the Lord GOD, "that I will send a famine on the land, not a famine of bread, nor a thirst for water, but of hearing the words of the LORD. They shall wander from sea to sea, and from north to east; they shall run to and fro, seeking the word of the LORD, but shall not find it."

Amos 8:11–12

It was harvest time in Israel, and the vineyards should have been bursting with fruit. According to Micah, there were no clusters hanging from the vines. He watched as people went into the vineyards looking for fruit to pick but finding none. A literal famine had swept the land, mirroring the spiritual famine among God's people. Now Micah was voicing the corporate cry of every hungry soul: "My soul desires fruit from the vine, true spiritual food. But there is none to be found."

As Micah uttered these words, he spoke also for another hungry people—the Church of Jesus Christ in these last days. In his prophetic eye, Micah saw multitudes in the last days running from place to place, seeking to hear a true word from God. He envisioned believers scurrying from church to church, from revival to revival, from nation to nation—all seeking to satisfy a hunger and thirst for something to nourish their souls. The cry is still heard, "Woe is me! There is no cluster."

Our ministry sees the fulfillment of Micah's prophecy in many of the letters we receive. One woman wrote: "Brother David, my church is growing in numbers, but it's dying spiritually. Our pastor used to preach an anointed message, with Holy Spirit power and authority. But somehow he got caught up in a new contemporary gospel that features skits and short, inoffensive sermonettes. He came back from a conference a changed man, and since then the goal in our church has been not to offend outsiders who come through the doors."

She continued: "Our pastor never mentions sin now from the pulpit. Instead, he reads a fifteen-minute message—a very light, shallow gospel provided by the conference he attended. Now we have a one-hour service that's lifeless and dead. All the power is gone. I'm convinced I have to leave, because I'm starving. But where can I go? Most other places I have attended are just as dead, or they are into entertainment."

I received a call from someone who told me a disturbing true story about the pastor of a large contemporary church. During one worship service, the music team sang a medley of choruses on the blood of Christ. As the pastor sat listening, his face grew red. After the service, he called the worship team into his office and in a rage he cried, "If I ever hear a song on the blood again, I'll fire you on the spot. Visitors to this church don't understand what the blood means, and we are not going to offend them by singing about it."

Both of these reports reflect Micah's prophecy concerning our day: There is a great famine in the land. Yet, in spite of these multitudes running about looking for spiritual food, those who truly desire God's Word comprise only a remnant (see Micah 7:14, 18). This is certainly as true today as it was for ancient Israel. Few Christians today truly hunger to hear the pure Word of the Lord. Instead, the majority fatten themselves on Sodom's apples, feeding on the straw of perverted gospels.

My heart goes out to every person who has been snared by soulish revivals, or the bloodless, powerless, contemporary gospel. Tragically, one day these multitudes will stand before God's judgment seat unprepared. They have never been confronted about their sins or heard the convicting word of truth that would produce Christ's character in them. They have been given nothing with which to build their spiritual house except wood, hay and stubble. And when they are called to stand before Jesus, everything they have built their foundation upon will burn. What an awful moment that will be for them!

Some pastors are deeply offended when I speak of compromising churches and backslidden shepherds. Yet I believe no godly minister could possibly be offended by this if he is preaching under the anointing of the Holy Spirit. Those who seek God and share the burden of the Lord in Christ's true Church would have to agree that there is only a remnant left holding to biblical principles and preaching.

The Lord has spoken a searing indictment against all ministers who seek to accommodate sinners: "They continually say to those who despise Me, 'The LORD has said, "You shall have peace"'; and to everyone who walks according to the dictates of his own heart, they say, 'No evil shall come upon you'" (Jeremiah 23:17).

> "They prophesied by Baal and caused My people Israel to err. . . . 'From the prophets of Jerusalem profaneness has gone out into all the land.' . . . I have not sent these prophets, yet they ran. I have not spoken to them, yet they prophesied. But if they had stood in My counsel, and had caused My people to hear My words, then they would have turned them from their evil way and from the evil of their doings."
>
> Jeremiah 23:13, 15, 21–22

Encroaching Worldliness

According to Micah, Israel's spiritual famine could not have come at a worse time—at the height of the nation's moral decay. Israel's society had become depraved and corrupt. The time was ripe for a righteous testimony and a loving rebuke to the nation's leaders for their sin. Yet at the very moment this should have been happening, the nation was becoming more worldly. God's people were so caught up in greed and lust, they were powerless to expose sin.

Micah lists the nation's awful corruptions in chapter 7—a list that mirrors today's headlines:

Greed Is Growing

"The faithful man has perished from the earth, and there is no one upright among men. They all lie in wait for blood; every man hunts his brother with a net" (Micah 7:2).

According to Micah, the day had vanished when a man's word was his bond. The same is true today. I remember a time when honest, upright men made deals with a mere handshake—and that simple bond was as good as a written, signed contract. Today, however, the common creed is, "Every man for himself." Everyone is out to get his piece of the pie. And the phrase "blood money" has never been more relevant, with people bent on destroying whoever stands in their way. We no longer hear, "How can I contribute? What can I do to help?" Instead, the cry is, "What's in it for me? What will I get out of it?"

Because of these attitudes, our streets are now crawling with greedy schemers who are out to rob elderly people of their savings. Men disguise themselves as repairmen or masquerade as telephone solicitors to try to talk unsuspecting people into spending their last dollar. They use scams to steal homes from widows and cast them onto the street.

Once Respectable Figures Are Selling Out

"That they may successfully do evil with both hands—the prince asks for gifts, the judge seeks a bribe, and the great man utters his evil desire; so they scheme together" (Micah 7:3).

Politicians and judges—supposedly respectable figures in our society—have put their integrity up for sale. They regularly extend both hands for bribes, weaving complicated schemes to satisfy their greed. If the bribe is big enough, they will even sell out their own families.

"Every man has his price"—this phrase applies today more than ever. The wheels of society are greased by payoffs, especially in major cities. You can ask any construction manager, anyone in the building trade or anyone in city government or commerce. They know that many are willing to sell out for bribes.

God's Judgment Is Near

"The day of your watchman and your punishment comes; now shall be their perplexity" (Micah 7:4).

The warnings of God's watchmen are about to be fulfilled. We know this because we see their words beginning to come to pass in our own day. Just as Micah warned, we live in a time of unprecedented wickedness. Perplexity and confusion have fallen on every nation, and now the Lord is about to vindicate the words of His praying prophets. If He did not verify their warnings by His almighty judgments, eventually no one would listen. That is why His visitation is near; in fact, it is almost upon us.

Trust Is Broken at Every Level

"Do not trust in a friend; do not put your confidence in a companion; guard the doors of your mouth from her who lies in your bosom" (Micah 7:5).

Soon few people will be able to trust their friends and there will be a worsening breakdown of family structures. Jesus Himself said that a man's enemies would become those of his own household (see Matthew 10:36). Already we see a lack of trust between spouses, rampant divorce, a loss of parental authority, children becoming a law unto themselves, families taking each other to court.

Scripture tells us that at one point in Israel, "Everyone did what was right in his own eyes" (Judges 21:25). Many nations are at that point right now. People no longer trust their leaders, their governments, their judicial systems. They do not trust their employers, their coworkers, their friends—and they do not trust religion. We are seeing a breakdown of trust at every level of our society.

Isaiah was a contemporary of Micah, and he verified the moral landslide his fellow prophet described. Both men preached to the same generation, reinforcing each other's prophecies. Isaiah's words here paint a similar picture of utter moral decay:

> Alas, sinful nation, a people laden with iniquity, a brood of evildoers, children who are corrupters! They have forsaken the LORD, they have provoked to anger the Holy One of Israel, they have turned away backward. . . . From the sole of the foot even to the head, there is no soundness in it, but wounds and bruises and putrefying sores.
>
> Isaiah 1:4, 6

THE REST OF THE PICTURE

Up to this point, Micah has shown us only part of the last-days picture—now he proceeds to show us the rest of the story.

"Therefore I will look to the LORD; I will wait for the God of my salvation; my God will hear me" (Micah 7:7). Micah's use of the word *therefore* here means "in light of." He is saying, "In light of all this decay and ruin, I'm going to look to the Lord. I'm going to seek Him in prayer, and wait on Him in confidence and trust."

As Micah read the times, he faithfully pointed out the moral decay plaguing Israel. Now he turned his gaze away from all the decadence, greed and covetousness in the society. He stopped focusing on the backsliding and compromising and he told Israel, in essence, "Yes, there is a spiritual famine in the land. We are in the midst of a moral landslide beyond that of any generation in history. Depravity is plaguing our nation's soul, causing ruin and decay, and the foolishness taking place among God's people is an abomination in God's sight. We watchmen are fully aware of it all. That's why we reprove it and warn about it. We cry out faithfully so that every hearer is prepared for judgment.

"But ultimately, our focus is not on the awful condition of society. You see, a true watchman doesn't just warn of the sword, he also proclaims the covenant promises of God. Our focus in speaking these things isn't to scare you by prophesying what is coming. Rather, it is to prepare you for it all. And to do that, we will speak to you about God's plan for His people in the midst of the chaos. He wants His holy remnant to know His heart toward them."

Micah was speaking here for the holy remnant. He was voicing the outlook of those who had turned from the pleasures and pursuits of this world and instead were spending time seeking God's face. Likewise today, the Lord has a remnant whose eyes are not focused on the coming depression or the ruin of the Church. They are aware of it all, because the Lord's watchmen have faithfully warned of it. But they are preoccupied instead with the true focus of God's spokesmen: "Turn your attention away from all the decay you see around you, and turn your eyes toward the Lord. Seek His face, and wait on Him. He will sustain you and meet all your needs."

Next, Micah addressed Israel's enemies with a warning:

> Do not rejoice over me, my enemy; when I fall, I will arise; when I sit in darkness, the LORD will be a light to me. I will bear the

indignation of the LORD, because I have sinned against Him, until He pleads my case and executes justice for me. He will bring me forth to the light; I will see His righteousness.

Micah 7:8–9

I ask you: Who can say to Satan, our enemy, as Micah did, "That's enough—you cannot frighten me or chain me. The Lord promises to be a light to me in all things, including these dark times"? Such words are used only by the remnant believer who has turned totally to the Lord—who is on his knees, seeking God and waiting on Him. The Lord has empowered him mightily to take authority over the powers of hell, and this person can testify: "Even if I should fall, I will rise up again. When the devil tries to cast darkness over me, accusing me of past sins, the Lord will be a light to me. Satan, you can't hold me with your lies anymore. I have acknowledged my sins, and I have a High Priest, Jesus, pleading my case. You say I'm not righteous, but He has sworn by covenant oath to bring me through to victory by His own righteousness."

Maybe the devil is trying to heap guilt on you about a sin you are still battling. Micah writes, "Then she who is my enemy will see, and shame will cover her who said to me, 'Where is the LORD your God?' My eyes will see her; now she will be trampled down like mud in the streets" (Micah 7:10). The prophet is saying, in other words: "Satan may come to you accusing, 'Where is your victory over sin? You're still having problems, still being tempted mightily. Why won't your covenant God help you? After all, He made all of those promises to deliver you.'"

Micah declares that you no longer have to be taunted by the principalities and powers of hell. The prophet states, "In the day when your walls are to be built, in that day the decree shall go far and wide" (Micah 7:11). Micah is giving us the reply of the remnant: "So, devil—you ask where my covenant God is and I'll tell you. He's building holy walls of protection around me."

"'For I,' says the LORD, 'will be a wall of fire all around her, and I will be the glory in her midst'" (Zechariah 2:5). What are the walls that Zechariah is describing here? They are walls of truth—the glorious truth of God's delivering power, as revealed in His New Covenant. The Lord promises, "I will build up your walls and dwell as the glory therein. The devil won't be able to climb over, dig under or get in by any other way. You will be protected by My walls of truth."

PROMISES FOR THESE TROUBLED TIMES

The covenant promises Micah begins to reveal at this point seem too incredible to be true. Yet I want to prove to you that all of these promises are intended for the Church of Jesus Christ in these present times.

We find our proof in Micah 7:14: "Shepherd Your people with Your staff, the flock of Your heritage, who dwell solitarily in a woodland." The original Hebrew in Spurrell's text reads: "Shepherd thy sheep with thy rod." David tells us that the shepherd is "You who dwell between the cherubim" (Psalm 80:1). The author of Hebrews writes: "Our Lord Jesus . . . that great Shepherd of the sheep, through the blood of the everlasting covenant" (Hebrews 13:20). And Isaiah says: "He will feed His flock like a shepherd; He will gather the lambs with His arm, and carry them in His bosom, and gently lead those who are with young" (Isaiah 40:11). This Shepherd is none other than Jesus Christ.

Now, we know that the incarnated Jesus did not feed sheep in the Old Covenant. I believe, therefore, that Micah's statement refers to the covenant that God cut with His Son in eternity. It stipulated that Jesus would come to earth to shepherd and feed the flock. God promised at that point, "There will never be a famine for those who turn to Me in faith and trust."

What does all this tell us about the present famine? It says we cannot always blame our lack of bread solely on dead churches or unconcerned pastors. I know personally of some Christians who would not be happy even in a church pastored by the apostle Paul. I say to all such believers who have judgmental attitudes: You will never find a place of worship to suit you if you are not on your knees daily, seeking God's face and regularly digging into His Word.

Are you looking for a church to provide your spiritual joy? If you are looking to sources other than the Lord Himself, you will never find real food. But if you will turn to Him, He promises by oath to feed you. This pledge is good even to those who live in solitary places, where there may be no church: "Who dwell solitarily in a woodland" (Micah 7:14).

DAYS OF DELIVERANCE

In the next verse we find one of the most glorious promises God ever made to His people: His pledge to give us our own personal Red Sea deliverance. "As in the days when you came out of the land of Egypt, I will show them wonders" (Micah 7:15).

Micah is referring here to the miracle that God performed for Israel at the Red Sea. He is prophesying that this promise extends to His Church in these last days. That is right—the Lord pledges to do something equally awesome for us today. He is saying, "I am going to do for you in the Spirit what I did for Israel in the natural. You are going to experience your own Red

Sea miracle. The Israelites were helpless against their adversary, Pharaoh. They had no possible way to deliver themselves from his masses of troops, so I took their deliverance into My own hands. I made their way of escape, drowning all those soldiers in the sea.

"Today your adversary is Satan and his troops of demons. He is coming against you, just as he did against Israel through Pharaoh. Your enemy is determined to bring you back into captivity, binding and enslaving you. But I will deliver My people once again. I will take your deliverance into My own hands, and, if you will trust Me, you will see your adversary crushed under My heel. You will watch in awe as your sins sink to the bottom of the sea, just as Pharaoh's soldiers did."

Scripture sums up Israel's miracle this way:

> He rebuked the Red Sea also, and it dried up; so He led them through the depths, as through the wilderness. He saved them from the hand of him who hated them, and redeemed them from the hand of the enemy. The waters covered their enemies; there was not one of them left.
>
> Psalm 106:9–11

Isaiah as well describes God's promise to us of our very own Red Sea deliverance:

> "I am the LORD, your Holy One, the Creator of Israel, your King." Thus says the LORD, who makes a way in the sea and a path through the mighty waters, who brings forth the chariot and horse, the army and the power (they shall lie down together, they shall not rise; they are extinguished, they are quenched like a wick): "Do not remember the former things, nor consider the things of old."
>
> Isaiah 43:15–18

In so many words, God is telling us through Isaiah, "For years you have heard sermons about the great miracle I performed at the Red Sea. Yet as wonderful as that deliverance was, it was only a type, a shadow. I want you to see beyond all that—because I am going to do a totally new thing for you." The next verse says: "Behold, I will do a new thing, now it shall spring forth; shall you not know it? I will even make a road in the wilderness and rivers in the desert" (Isaiah 43:19).

Right now you are in a spiritual wilderness, facing the powers of Satan. You can feel his army of demonic entities thundering down on you. Just as the Israelites were helpless against their enemy, you are helpless against yours. You have made all the promises to God you can make, and you have failed every one of them.

But just as surely as God opened the Red Sea, allowing Israel to walk through on dry ground, He is going to open up your sea supernaturally. You are going to walk through your besetting sin—through all of the devil's opposition. God is going to take you through your own Red Sea experience, so you will no longer have to fear the enemy.

Micah prophesied, "The nations shall see and be ashamed of all their might; they shall put their hand over their mouth; their ears shall be deaf" (Micah 7:16). The Hebrew root word for *nations* has a figurative meaning of "goy"—which in turn means "a troop of crawling animals, vipers." Micah is saying, "God's people are going to grow strong through the revelation that He keeps His promises to His remnant. When they realize He has delivered them from the dominion of sin, they will be imbued with joy. This in turn will build their faith, releasing in them such strength that they will become fearless. In fact, the manifestation of Holy Spirit power in them will confound and frighten their enemy, the devil. It will stupefy all his creeping, demonic entities."

In the devil's kingdom I was so used to always working, working, working, trying to earn his favor and move up in the ranks. When I came to Christ I often caught myself trying to earn God's love in the same way.

My family was engulfed in witchcraft for generations. When I was ten years old I was sworn into the occult by my mother and my next 25 years were pure hell. I became the third-highest ranked warlock in New York City.

Someone invited me to attend church and I accepted out of curiosity. During the service, demons overtook me and I attacked the pastor. Many in the congregation quickly sprang to his rescue and pried my claws off his throat. After things settled down, I was shocked when people came up and showed me the love of Jesus. I went home pondering, "Why would these people love me when I am a son of Satan?" For months I was tormented, caught between two worlds—committed to the satanic realm, yet being pulled by the love of Jesus.

One night in desperation I was ready to end it all. I sat on my bed and told God I wanted nothing more to do with Him or Jesus. I thought that settled it, but as I was falling asleep, I heard these words come out of my mouth: "Jesus, if You are bigger than the devil, You show me tonight." Then I fell into a deep sleep.

Through a bigger-than-life dream of Jesus Christ, I awoke to a new life at the foot of the cross. I accepted Jesus as my Lord and Savior, not knowing He could forgive a sinner like me. In an instant, He broke the generational curse of witchcraft and delivered me from a life of debauchery, sorcery and demonic contracts. I was set free!

The Lord led me to Times Square Church, where I found the heart of God through Pastor David Wilkerson and his sermons. His teachings on the New Covenant impacted my life in a powerful way. Before I came to TSC I was perplexed, because in the devil's kingdom I was so used to always working, working, working, trying to earn his favor and move up in the ranks. When I came to Christ I often caught myself trying to earn God's love in the same way.

Thank God that Pastor David unveiled the New Covenant and showed us that through God's love, mercy and grace, we do not have to try to achieve things by works. We just need to embrace what Jesus did for us at the cross and trust His finished work.

—John

Your Red Sea deliverance is going to silence Satan's lies. He will have to "cover his mouth" in awe as God's Spirit moves in you. You will no longer believe his accusations against you. Instead, his demonic principalities and powers will end up confused.

What Are Strongholds?

Many Christians quote 2 Corinthians 10:3-4: "We do not war according to the flesh. For the weapons of our warfare are not carnal but mighty in God for pulling down strongholds." Most of us think of strongholds as bondages such as sexual trespasses, drug addictions, alcoholism—outward sins we put at the top of a "worst sins" list. But Paul is referring here to something much worse than our human measuring of sins.

First of all, he is not speaking of demonic possession. In my opinion, the devil cannot enter the heart of any overcoming Christian and claim a place in that person. Rather, the figurative meaning of Paul's word *stronghold* in Greek here is "holding firmly to an argument." A stronghold is an accusation planted firmly in your mind. *Satan establishes strongholds in God's people by implanting in their minds falsehoods and misconceptions, especially regarding God's nature.*

For instance, the enemy may plant in your mind the lie that you are unspiritual—unworthy of God's grace. He may whisper to you repeatedly, "You will never be free of your besetting sin. You haven't tried hard enough. You are a phony Christian because your mind is still full of evil thoughts. You haven't changed, and God has lost patience with you because of your continual ups and downs. You aren't worthy to receive any more of His grace. You're just not spiritual—and you never will be."

Or, the devil may try to convince you that you have a right to hold on to bitterness because you have been wronged. He will try to destroy your marriage by persuading you, "You can't endure this relationship any longer unless your spouse changes." If you keep listening to his lies, you will begin to believe them after a while. *And once you buy his evil argument, it will become embedded in your mind and heart—and then it will become a stronghold.* This will keep Satan empowered over you through your thought life. He does not have to possess your body; all he needs is a foothold in your mind. Soon you will not be able to worship or praise God anymore, because his "worm" of a lie will constantly twist and turn in your mind, tormenting your thoughts.

This explains why so many Christians are under harassment from hell right now. Satan is the accuser of the brethren, coming against us time after time with his army of accusers, planting demonic lies in our minds. He even mimics the voice of God, misquoting the Scriptures to try to convince us of falsehoods about ourselves and the Lord. These lies are his strongholds, and if we do not resist them by God's Word they will turn into embedded fears in our minds.

We cannot pull down these strongholds by prayer alone. Nor can we pull them down by having some preacher prophesy over us or try to cast them out through physical manifestations. Satan is not impressed with any manifestation, or with loud shouting, or even with our goodness. The only weapon that scares the devil and his armies is the same one that scared him in the wilderness temptations of Jesus. That weapon is the truth of the New Covenant—the living Word of God. Only the Lord's truth can set us free. He promises to be God to us . . . to cleanse us, forgive us and cast away all our sins . . . to fill us with His Spirit . . . to lead, instruct and guide us by His Spirit and put within us all the power we need to walk in holiness and obedience.

According to Micah, here is the promise we are to cling to:

Who is a God like You, pardoning iniquity and passing over the transgression of the remnant of His heritage? He does not retain His anger forever, because He delights in mercy. He will again have compassion on us, and will subdue our iniquities. You will cast all our sins into the depths of the sea.

Micah 7:18–19

In Hebrew, the word *subdue* means "to trample on." We do not subdue our sins; *He* will subdue them. Our Lord is going to have compassion on us, trampling all our iniquities under-foot. He will cast them into the sea, never to be held against us again. Think of the children of Israel watching all those Egyptian soldiers disappear into the water forever. Now the Lord is telling us, "Those are your sins and you are going to watch them sink to the bottom of the sea. I am going to drown them all and wash them away for good."

ABOLISHING YOUR FEARS

If you will lay hold of these covenant promises, God pledges that the enemy will be scattered before your eyes. "They shall lick the dust like a serpent; they shall crawl from their holes like snakes of the earth. They shall be afraid of the LORD our God, and shall fear because of You" (Micah 7:17). The word for *worms* in Hebrew here means, figuratively, "crawling, creeping serpentine fears." *These worms Micah refers to are Satan's planted fears—accusations embedded in the mind. And God says they are going to "crawl out of their holes."*

What does this mean? The Hebrew word for *hole* comes from the root word *cagar*, meaning "stronghold." The root of this same word means "to surrender." Putting these two meanings together, the verse says, "All satanic lies are going to surrender, moving out of their strongholds." Simply put, when you stand on the covenant promises of God, every demonic power is going to surrender its stronghold. They are all going to crawl out of your mind in fear of almighty God.

Not only will these devilish strongholds in your mind surrender but, in addition, the devil and his whole army "shall be afraid of the Lord our God, and shall fear" because of Him. You will no longer be afraid of the devil; instead, he is going to be afraid of you. He fears every believer who walks in the almighty Deliverer's promises of His everlasting New Covenant.

God is faithful to fulfill His promise to cause every enemy to flee from us. Think of Israel standing on the Egyptian side of the Red Sea. The enemy was closing in, trapping God's people, allowing no way of escape. Do not think that at that point God said to them, "I'm sorry, Israel—I can't deliver you. You have thousands of little golden idols packed away in your luggage.

You have to get rid of your idolatry before I'll bring deliverance. Otherwise, you're as good as dead."

The very thought that God would respond in this way is impossible. What kind of God would refuse to deliver His own people because they still struggled with a lust?

God will not abandon you at your Red Sea. Your temptations, habits and besetting sins may look like impossible roadblocks before you, but the Lord promises to deliver you, for His own name's sake. Our God is faithful to keep His covenant.

Make this your prayer: "Lord, You have promised by oath to be God to me. You have said You would give me my own Red Sea experience. You have also said the devil would have to put his hand over his mouth and no longer be able to accuse me with his lies. I stand on Your covenant promises now, Father. Deliver me—and glorify Yourself in my life."

DISCUSSION QUESTIONS

1. Micah 7 is a powerful message on the New Covenant. What was Micah describing that was happening in Israel? (Page 137)

2. Through prophetic insight, Micah foresaw the last days. What did he see? (Page 138)

3. The prophet Micah lists the corruption of the nation of Israel in Micah 7. Micah's list is a mirror image of today's society. List the four main corruptions of Micah 7:2–5. (Pages 141–142)

4. Micah was not just speaking about the dreadful spiritual and moral famine in Israel, but was bringing a

powerful word of comfort to those whose hearts were hungry to follow God. In your own words explain Micah's teaching and proclamation. (Pages 143–146)

5. As Micah 7:15–16 speaks to the deliverance of the children of Israel from Egypt, how does it apply to the Last Days' Church? (Pages 147–148)

6. What is the apostle Paul's definition of the word *stronghold*? (Page 152)

7. Strongholds are "pulled down" in what two ways? (Page 153)

8. God promises to "subdue" our iniquities. In your own words explain how the promise of Micah 7:18–19 applies to us and to the Last Days' Church. (Page 155)

10

THE NEW COVENANT AND THE SECRET OF THE LORD

"The secret of the LORD is with those who fear Him, and He will show them His covenant" (Psalm 25:14).

I believe God carefully chose the word *secret* to use in this passage. Its Hebrew root means "to be alert, to be on the lookout, to watch, to be a confidant." The concept being expressed here is powerful: God has a secret He will share only with believers who are willing to pursue it with passion. This company of seekers will become His confidants only by having a deep hunger to know His heart.

In essence, the Lord does not share His secret with just anybody, even within the Body of Christ. Flippant Christians will not grasp it, and casual believers will never enter into it. The Bible calls it a secret because it is for His confidants only.

I believe this secret of the covenant is a lifeline God casts toward every Christian who is sinking in a mire of sin. Through it, He calls out to every child bound by a lust, habit or evil strong-hold, saying, "Lay hold of My covenant. It will be a lifeline to you, providing an escape from sin before you are swept away."

Yet—I say this as kindly as possible—only a handful of Christians will grasp this lifeline. A believer can memorize all the glorious promises of the New Covenant, master complex theological outlines and trace each of the biblical covenants from the Adamic to the New. But only a few will set their minds to seek the Lord diligently for understanding of His life-giving New Covenant.

In review, here are just a few of the promises and provisions God gives us through the New Covenant: a new heart, a righteous fear of God, dominion over sin, Holy Spirit mortification of all sin within us, a heart to know the Lord, His Law written within our hearts so we will not sin against Him. God also pledges that we will be taught by His own Spirit, kept from falling and caused to walk in His ways, do His good pleasure and endure to the end—all through the abiding power of the Holy Spirit.

You may reason, "If God has decreed the covenant—if He has sworn an oath to do these wonderful things, and His Word is unchangeable—why should I pray for what He has already decreed? Why should I ask Him to deliver me, when He has already pledged to do for me what I cannot do for myself? Shouldn't I just wait on Him in faith? If His covenant promises are binding, why should I believe there are conditions attached to them, such as prayer and diligent seeking?"

In response, let me ask you: Why would Jesus, who made the covenant with His Father, pray diligently, as He did so often? In fact, why would He ask the Father three times for an answer to a single matter? And why would He praise a woman in a parable who kept pestering a judge until she got the verdict she wanted?

I hope to prove to you in this chapter that God has hung the secret of the covenant upon the condition of seeking Him with all our hearts. This condition and its accompanying disciplines—prayer, Bible study, diligent seeking—cannot in any way merit the covenant promises for us. But they do prepare our hearts to receive what God has promised. Let me explain.

GLORIOUS PROMISES

Ezekiel 36 gives us some of the most glorious promises of the New Covenant.

> "Then I will sprinkle clean water on you, and you shall be clean; I will cleanse you from all your filthiness and from all your idols. I will give you a new heart and put a new spirit within you; I will take the heart of stone out of your flesh and give you a heart of flesh. I will put My Spirit within you and cause you to walk in My statutes, and you will keep My judgments and do them."
>
> Ezekiel 36:25–27

God is making us an ironclad promise: "You will be clean, I swear it—free of all filthiness, guilt and shame. You no longer have to live under a black cloud of dread and despair. You no longer have to fear exposure and loss." Also, the last verse in this passage contains a New Covenant promise that I believe is the very gate to heaven on earth: God swears to put His Spirit within us, causing us to obey His Word and do His commands.

Do you understand the implications of this message for your life? God wants to share with you the secret of His life-giving, soul-freeing covenant. He wants you to lay hold of a truth that will cut off all your chains. So—are you still hooked by a secret sin? Is your mind riddled with lustful thoughts? Are you gripped by a besetting sin you know is defiling God's temple, your body? Are you wrestling with a habit—drug use, secret drinking, fornication, adultery, homosexuality, bitterness, unforgiveness? The Lord says His covenant is your passport to victory—to gaining dominion over your sin.

Now He gives you this condition: "'I, the LORD, have spoken it, and I will do it.' Thus says the Lord GOD: 'I will also let the house of Israel inquire of Me to do this for them'" (Ezekiel 36:36–37).

Just prior to this verse, the Lord enumerates the covenant promises, and now He decrees that all of those blessings are tied directly to seeking Him. He is saying, in essence, "I have made an oath to you that cannot be broken. I'm going to cast your sins into the sea, so that you are never threatened by them again. And I'm going to send My Spirit to sanctify you and change your heart. All of the promised blessings will be yours and, finally, these things will be freely given to everyone who diligently seeks Me."

Why would the Lord attach this last condition? The Bible clearly states that it is God's will for all people to be saved. Yet His Word also says, "I desire therefore that the men pray everywhere" (1 Timothy 2:8). God wills both salvation for His people and prayer from His people. When He says, "I will also let the house of Israel inquire of Me to do this for them" (Ezekiel 36:37), the literal Hebrew meaning is, "I am tying the revelation of My covenant to this condition—that you seek Me with all your heart. If you do this with all diligence, I will share with you the secret of My covenant."

I can personally testify that this is just what God did for me. After years of reading about the covenant, my eyes were not opened until I began to fast and pray with all diligence. These prayers and fasts were not meant to merit anything from the

> **From the vantage point of God's unchanging grace, we are able to see potential in our lives where otherwise we might see only abject and irredeemable failure.**

The first time I heard Pastor David Wilkerson speak, I was a homeless, 23-year-old lost soul. Wandering aimlessly through the streets of New York City, hopeless and lonely, I slept in parks and subways at night and viewed the world through a haze of despondency and despair. One day as I walked along a side street in Times Square, my head clouded in gloom, someone invited me to church. I was so tired that I figured at least I would get to sit down for a while.

I had been in church many times during my childhood and teen years, but my experiences had not been pleasant ones.

I did not know of David Wilkerson or his ministry, but I knew instinctively that he actually believed what he preached and that he based his life on it. My heart leapt as I realized that God had met my need.

Pastor Dave's insight into God's covenant faithfulness impacted me more than anything. Because of his unique perspective into the heart of God, he could see people from the vantage point of God's unchanging grace. He saw potential in lives (and my life!) where many would have seen only abject and irredeemable failure.

He was convinced that God had promised to completely change the hearts of all who accepted His invitation to new life. Because God had given him insight into this promise, he could see pimps become preachers and pushers become pastors. He was able to visualize prostitutes prophesying and gangsters glorifying God. And in my case, he was able to see a helpless young man through the eyes of God's Covenant promise.

My first opportunity to serve, my first academic opportunity, my first pastoral responsibility—all were initiated in his office. Because Pastor Dave embraced New Covenant grace, I am forever changed and forever grateful.

—William

Lord or to earn His favor, however. I fasted and prayed because I was desperate to have my understanding opened to His secret. I knew that God was waiting until I set my heart to seek Him—and that I would not let go until He showed me His covenant.

We see this pattern all through the Scriptures: God says, "I give you these promises—but I want you to seek My face until you are fully persuaded of them." There has never been a time, from the foundation of the world, when God's people were not under a covenant. Yet, godly men and women have fasted and prayed throughout the centuries, holding the Lord to His Word. The Bible gives us several examples of this.

1. In the book of Judges, Israel made war against the Benjamites with a righteous cause.

A group of Benjamites had raped a Levite's concubine and attempted to homosexually rape the Levite himself. Now the Israelites, in going to war, knew they stood on solid ground. They held on to the covenant promise that assured God's favor toward those who would remove wickedness from the land.

Yet when the Israelites attacked Benjamin—twice—they failed both times. As they regrouped for a third attempt, they realized they needed more to obtain victory than merely a just cause. Scripture tells us:

> All the children of Israel, that is, all the people, went up and came to the house of God and wept. They sat there before the LORD and fasted that day until evening; and they offered burnt offerings and peace offerings before the LORD.
>
> Judges 20:26

Through prayer and fasting, they remembered the covenant. Only after fasting and seeking the Lord diligently did the Israelites overcome their enemy. They were victorious—and God fulfilled every covenant promise He made to them, because their renewed understanding of covenant now produced faith in them.

> 2. *Jacob was given a sure promise by God through the Abrahamic covenant.*

The Lord had promised to be his shield, so no one could harm him. Furthermore, God had assured him, "Return to your country and to your family, and I will deal well with you" (Genesis 32:9). What powerful promises these were! Who could oppose a man whose God was with him, as Jacob's was?

Still, Jacob was compelled to pray the covenant. He cried out, "Lord, You promised to deal well with me if I returned. Now I'm holding You to that promise" (see Genesis 32:10–12). Scripture tells us Jacob then wrestled all night with an angel of the Lord. He told the Lord, "I will not let You go unless You bless me!" (Genesis 32:26). He was holding the Lord to His covenant.

> 3. *When the Israelites were taken captive by Babylon and put under bondage, God gave His people a covenant promise.*

He told them that after seventy years they would return to Jerusalem and rebuild their capital and nation. Later, when exactly seventy years had passed, God stirred the heart of Babylon's King Cyrus and moved him to send the Israelites back to their homeland. So Ezra led a host of Israelites out of Babylon, with this covenant promise ringing in their ears: "The hand of our God is upon all those for good who seek Him" (Ezra 8:22).

At that point, Ezra stopped the procession and called the people to prayer and fasting. He writes, "Then I proclaimed a fast there . . . that we might humble ourselves before our God, to seek from Him the right way for us and our little ones and all our possessions. . . . So we fasted and entreated our God for this, and He answered our prayer" (Ezra 8:21, 23).

Ezra knew that Israel had an ironclad covenant oath from God, yet he led all of Israel in fasting and prayer for a renewed revelation of covenant security. No one in Israel objected, saying, "We have the promise—let's move on." All were willing to seek the Lord diligently for what He had promised them.

> 4. *Jesus not only knew the covenant promises, having made covenant with the Father, but He was the New Covenant personified. All the covenant promises resided in Him. Yet even Jesus Himself fasted and prayed.*

At one point, a group of desperate people brought a demon-possessed, lunatic young man to Jesus. His disciples had not been able to cast out the demonic spirit, but when Jesus rebuked the devil, the demon immediately left the young man. The Bible says, "The child was cured from that very hour" (Matthew 17:18).

Jesus' disciples were perplexed. Scripture tells us, "Then the disciples came to Jesus privately and said, 'Why could we not cast it out?' So Jesus said to them, 'Because of your unbelief. . . . However, this kind does not go out except by prayer and fasting'" (Matthew 17:19–21).

Think of the implications of what Jesus is saying here. He is implying that if His disciples had spent time in prayer and fasting, they would have had both the faith and the power for the boy to be delivered. He also implied, "Yes, I had the power to cast out this demon because I am God in flesh. Yet I also set an example for you, through My prayer and fasting."

5. Hosea tells us that God said of the tribe of Ephraim, "I have written for him the great things of My law, but they were considered a strange thing" (Hosea 8:12).

The Lord was saying here, "I showed My covenant to Ephraim, giving them a word of hope and deliverance. But they rejected My word as too complicated and difficult to understand. They ignored the very truth that was intended to free them, as if it were some strange doctrine."

So it is in the Church today. The truth of the New Covenant is now being unveiled throughout the world by pastors and teachers—but, like Ephraim, the majority of Christians shrug it off as some strange, complicated gospel. Their thinking is, "If a teaching isn't easy—if I can't learn it quickly—if it requires me to study, pray, seek and ask—I don't have time for it."

For this reason, God said to Ephraim, "It is time to seek the LORD, till He comes and rains righteousness on you" (Hosea 10:12). God was telling His people, "I am going to reveal to you My lovingkindness and righteousness. But before that happens, you must seek Me for the revelation."

6. Jeremiah 31 is known as the New Covenant chapter. Note the words God spoke to Jeremiah:

"They shall come with weeping, and with supplications I will lead them. I will cause them to walk by the rivers of waters, in a straight way in which they shall not stumble; for I am a Father to Israel, and Ephraim is My firstborn."

Jeremiah 31:9

This passage speaks of spiritual Israel, which represents the Body of Christ today. God is issuing a call to His Church, saying, "People are going to come to Me from all over the world with prayer and supplication—because I am stirring their hearts, wanting to reveal My Word to them. These holy ones will not stumble or fall. Instead, they will grow in grace, becoming more holy and righteous than any previous generation, in spite of the wickedness of society around them."

How does God promise to bring His confidants into this place of straight ways, where they will not fear stumbling or falling? He will do it through His covenant. The Holy Spirit will reveal to His people this truth in answer to their tender weeping and fervent, earnest prayer.

The Secret of the Lord

What is the secret God wants to share with His people? It is not just about the Holy Spirit coming into our hearts to break sin's dominion over us. His secret is about *how* the Spirit accomplishes this work. So, how does He do it?

We find an example in the life of Elijah. This man lived in a day when God's power was seen in thunder, lightning, storms, earthquakes—visible manifestations of mighty power. Elijah himself had been used to call down visible fire from heaven before four hundred prophets of Baal. But now, as we pick up the story, Elijah was running from God, discouraged and wanting to die. He ended up in a cave, in the throes of deep depression.

When the Lord found him there, He said, "Elijah, I want to speak to you." Then God showed the prophet His secret with a power greater than any manifestation Elijah had seen. What was this power? It was the still, small voice of a loving Father—a forgiving voice full of lovingkindness speaking to a downcast servant full of confusion.

God did not say, "Shame on you, Elijah; you have fallen too far, reproaching Me in the eyes of this heathen people. Now you're on your own until you wake up to your sin." Instead, the Lord said lovingly, "Elijah, what are you doing in this cave? I want you to gird yourself and get back to work." There was no harshness in these words. God's call to Elijah was meant to restore and redirect a man in the midst of seeming failure and deep despair.

Here is the secret of the New Covenant: It is not some sudden rush of supernatural power in us, enabling us to resist an overwhelming temptation. Rather, it is God's still, small voice, revealing His love to us in the midst of our failure and testing.

I want to illustrate this truth through several letters our ministry has received. One sister in Christ wrote: "Moral weakness and failure—that's me. I continually go back to my old sins. I don't want to hurt my Lord, and I pray for Him to keep me from going back. Yet at times I feel He is tired of my failing in this same area all the time. But the truth is, I never hear from Him in the midst of my temptation. I feel ostracized."

Now, contrast this letter with an email from a young man in Christ: "Last night I was in prayer, experiencing great anguish in my soul. I had failed my Lord and sinned. My heart was breaking inside. I cried before Him, but all I could think was that I had gone too far. I asked Him, 'How can You still love me? Do You, Lord? Or have I gone too far?' I cried out for a single word from Him to let me know He still loves me.

"Then, with perfect timing, your message arrived entitled *Keep Yourself in the Love of God*. I was so overwhelmed and awed by the love of the Lord as I read it, I immediately repented, and my heart was flushed with God's love. It has made me love Him so much more."

This young man now stands in awe of God's love, and his love for Jesus has grown deeper. Why? When it seemed Satan had won the battle, he received a revelation of God's forgiving love and restoring grace.

Without grasping this incredible secret, we simply cannot lay hold of the covenant, and we cannot do effective battle against the enemy of our souls. You may try to go up against Satan, thinking, "The Holy Spirit is in me. He has promised to empower me against the devil." Yet the supernatural infusion of power you expect to fill you does not come. And then, when it does not and you fail the Lord, you are tempted to give up on the covenant, thinking, "It doesn't work."

I ask you to please pray for the Holy Spirit to open your understanding of what I am about to say to you. This secret of the covenant can revolutionize your life and change your walk with Him forever.

The Difference Found in the New Covenant

The New Covenant promises that God will show mercy toward all our iniquities and unrighteousness. Yet this is not new; the Lord has always been merciful in all of the biblical covenants. What is different about the New Covenant is *how* God shows us His mercy: He sends His Spirit to empower us with a revelation of the almighty grace and lovingkindness of Jesus Christ, at the very lowest point of our Christian walk—even while we are sinking in guilt and failure.

Every Sunday in America, churches sing about amazing grace. Yet, in large part, the Body of Christ has yet to understand just how amazing God's grace to us is. Once again, let me illustrate.

Consider a Christian who has loved the Lord for years. He is a praying, faithful believer with a gentle spirit and the sweet presence of Jesus about him. But suddenly this godly saint is overwhelmed by a powerful temptation. He yields to it—and immediately he is drawn back into an old, besetting sin. Perhaps his bondage is an outburst of temper, or swarms of evil thoughts, or lukewarmness, or gross sins such as heavy drinking, fornication or adultery.

The devil then quickly attacks this Christian using the only real power he has against him: lies. He tries to convince the believer of the following:

1. He has sinned against the Light.

2. He has sinned too often after being convicted for so long.

3. He has sinned one too many times.

4. He has crossed a line and is now beyond God's mercy.

Here, at this crucial point, is where the secret of the New Covenant is revealed. Instead of condemning that Christian, the Holy Spirit woos him, saying, "Come back quickly to the sprinkling of Jesus' blood. Repent, and accept your forgiveness. Stay in the love of God. You are forgiven unconditionally. Return now to your walk with Me."

What is happening at this moment? The Holy Spirit is at work—revealing the love of God to that person, causing him to marvel at the Lord's mercy and grace. And in doing so, He is drawing him into a greater love for Jesus.

That is the keeping power of the Holy Spirit. When you are down and hurting—when you think you have crossed a line and it is all over for you—the Spirit comes in immediately to lift you up and bring you back into God's grace. Every bit of your sin has been paid for, no matter how awful it may be. How? Jesus paid the price in full. God said by covenant, "I am going to be merciful to your sins, and I have sent My Son to you as the seal of My covenant. Your fear tells you I have every right to damn you, but My covenant says My Son took upon Himself everything that would ever damn you. You are now free."

Here is what the covenant is all about. It is God's love message to His people, saying, "I love you so much, I will never let the devil have you. I won't let him take over your life, even when you fail Me. It is impossible for you ever to stray too far from My love. There is no place in heaven or earth where you can escape it."

You may not have experienced supernatural power before or during your temptation, but surely it has come to you afterward. The fact is, God causes every failure by His children to reveal His everlasting love—magnifying His mercy, melting our hearts, wooing us away from sin. And, in the end, we are brought to a place where we are so awed, melted and overwhelmed by His love, we refuse to grieve the One who has shown us such mercy and kindness.

How long do you think the devil will keep tempting you in your weak area, when each time you quickly run back to God's grace and fall more in love with Jesus? Do you think Satan wants to keep driving you into Christ's arms to find mercy, love and grace? No—the only sin he can tempt you with now is to attempt to turn you away from God's incredible love. That is where a hard heart comes from—not from falling back, but from continually rejecting God's love.

Now you can truly sing, "Amazing grace—how sweet the sound!" You know you deserve wrath, hell and rejection, but

God's Spirit has come to you, revealing lovingkindness, forgiveness and acceptance. "Oh, the love that drew salvation's plan! Oh, the grace that brought it down to man!"

The secret of the Lord is a life-freeing revelation of His lovingkindness toward us at the point of our failures. It is the Holy Spirit enduing us with a powerful revelation that nothing can separate us from the covenant love of God. He is not mad at you, so get your eyes off your sin and gladly receive the free access you still have to the Father, through the cross of Christ.

This secret is that your Savior wants you to rejoice and be glad—because your past, present and future sins have been taken away. Be glad—then you will be privy to His secret.

DISCUSSION QUESTIONS

1. What is the meaning of the word *secret* as it is used in Psalm 25:14? (Page 157)

2. God shares His secret only with those who are willing to do what? (Page 157)

3. What is the one condition that God has placed upon the secret of the covenant? (Page 159)

4. In Ezekiel 36:25–27 God is expressing His desire to share what? (Page 159)

5. Read Ezekiel 36:36–37. The blessings of the secret of the Lord are tied to what? (Page 160)

6. What is the secret of the Lord? (Page 167)

7. One example of how God accomplishes this work in us is through the life of the prophet Elijah. When Elijah got discouraged and hid in a cave, how did God speak to him? (Page 166)

8. Explain what the secret of the New Covenant is not. Explain what it is. (Page 167)

9. What does the New Covenant teach us about how God forgives? (Page 169)

11

The New Covenant and the Preventing Love of the Lord

"Thou preventest him with the blessings of goodness: thou settest a crown of pure gold on his head" (Psalm 21:3, KJV).

At first glance, this verse from a psalm by David is puzzling, especially the opening phrase: "Thou preventest him with the blessings of goodness." We usually associate the word *prevent* with a hindrance of some sort, not with blessings. In this sense, the modern translation of this verse would be, "The Lord hindered David with the blessings of goodness."

Yet in Scripture, the word for *prevent* means something completely different. It means "to anticipate, to precede, to foresee and fulfill in advance, to pay a debt before it is due." Furthermore, in almost every instance, it implies something of pleasure.

Isaiah gives us a glimpse of this kind of pleasure—the kind that comes when God anticipates a need and fulfills it ahead of time. The Lord says through Isaiah, "It shall come to pass that before they call, I will answer; and while they are still speaking, I will hear" (Isaiah 65:24). This verse provides us with an incredible picture of our Lord's love for us. Evidently, He is so anxious to bless us, so ready to fulfill His lovingkindness to us, that He cannot even wait for us to tell Him our needs. Instead, He jumps in and performs acts of mercy, grace and love toward us. And that is a supreme pleasure to Him.

This is just what David is saying in Psalm 21: "Lord, You pour out blessings and lovingkindness on me before I can even ask. And You offer more than I could even conceive of asking." David is referring to some awesome work that God performed for him in the spiritual realm—something that gave David victory over his enemies, answers to prayer, overcoming power and unspeakable joy. And God did it all before David could get to his prayer closet. The king was not even given a chance to unburden his heart—to offer praise, examine himself or present his request. Instead, he was given a surprising kindness beyond anything he could imagine. Once David finally did pour out his heart to God—beseeching Him for help and strength to battle his foes—he discovered that God had already made provision to defeat his enemies. David's victory was assured before he could even get near the battlefield.

Actually, when David wrote Psalm 21, he was speaking of a literal battle. This psalm is a companion to Psalm 20, both referring to a battle described in 2 Samuel 10. In the 2 Samuel passage, Israel's enemy, the Ammonites, hired Syrian battalions to wage war against David. David dispatched his military leader, Joab, and a choice army to meet the battalions at the nation's border. They defeated the Syrians soundly—Israel's victory was overwhelming—and the enemy fled in fear.

At that point, David rejoiced, thinking, "That's the end of the Syrians—we won't have to deal with them again. Our army dealt them a death blow." He wrote in Psalm 18, "I have wounded them, so that they could not rise; they have fallen under my feet" (verse 38).

Yet Scripture tells us, "When the Syrians saw that they had been defeated by Israel, they gathered together" (2 Samuel 10:15). Israel's enemy regrouped and immediately began plotting another, larger attack. This time they planned to come against Israel with great chariots of iron.

You probably realize this story is more than just a history of David's troubles with the Syrians. It is also about the followers of Jesus Christ today and our battle with Satan, the enemy of our souls. It is about a battle we thought we had won long ago—perhaps against a lust, a habit, a temptation we once defeated. At the time we thought, "All my fasting and praying over this matter has paid off. I've finally won the victory, by faith. That old temptation is dead, never to rise again. I won't have to be plagued by it anymore."

Yet God gives us this story in Scripture to reveal to us a crucial lesson: Every victory we win over the flesh and the devil will soon be followed by an even greater temptation and stronger attack.

The Battle Heats Up

Satan simply will not give up in his war against us. If we defeat him once, he will redouble his forces and come right back at us. And suddenly we are in a spiritual war we thought we had already won. Worse, now he comes at us with iron chariots—weapons and devices of greater force and intensity than we have ever known.

Scripture tells us, "The Syrians set themselves in battle array against David and fought with him" (2 Samuel 10:17). Suddenly,

David was facing the same old enemy—one he thought he had defeated soundly—and now that enemy was coming at him with more troops and mighty chariots of iron.

It is important to note that David was not living in sin at this time. He was a godly man who walked in the fear of the Lord. Yet David was also human—and he must have been awfully confused about what was happening. Why would God allow this enemy to come against him again?

Have you stood in David's shoes? Perhaps you have prayed, "Lord, all I want is to please You—to obey Your Word and do what is right. You know that I fast, I pray and I love Your Word, and I don't ever want to grieve You. So why am I being tempted so severely? Why am I facing this same battle with an old enemy? Why is the lust I thought was dead now coming back upon me with even greater force?"

We know David had a tender heart, and no doubt this godly man searched his soul, wondering if the Lord had allowed the attacks because of some wicked way in him. Was he being disobedient in some way? He probably thought, "Lord, this is troubling me. What are You trying to say to me? Am I being disciplined? Oh, God, I need Your strength through this."

Is this not what goes through our minds whenever we face an enemy we thought was defeated long ago? When an old, familiar temptation or character flaw rises up in us, we are startled, confused, scared. And we begin to wallow in self-examination: "What did I do wrong? Is there some evil root in me? How else could I be tempted in this same area over and over? I thought I had victory over this thing, but now I'm right back in a struggle for my soul. I must be a phony, a hypocrite—a dirty, rotten, filthy Christian." We end up crying out as David did: "Help, Lord—I'm troubled. I need a miracle. This is beyond me, and I need help. Please, God, rid me of this thing once and for all."

Suddenly, in the midst of his confusion and soul-searching, David remembered the covenant God had made with him:

> "The LORD tells you that He will make you a house. When your days are fulfilled and you rest with your fathers, I will set up your seed after you, who will come from your body, and I will establish his kingdom."
>
> 2 Samuel 7:11–12

God reminded David of this promise as he was going to war. He wanted to remove all fear from His beloved servant. While the devil was throwing every weapon in hell at David, the Lord was showing him that even before he entered battle he would emerge a victor. He said, "I am going to plant you and your seed, so you will never have to be pushed around by your enemies. The wicked will no longer afflict you, as they have in the past, because I am going to cut them off. Your house is going to stand forever. So, when the Syrians show up in their iron chariots, you don't have to be moved. You are going to come out of this battle standing."

David laid hold of these covenant promises, and the first thing he did was take his eyes off the oncoming enemy. Now he was no longer weeping about being in trouble, trying to understand why the struggle had come. Instead, he basked in the revelation of God's lovingkindness and testified, "He delivered me because He delighted in me" (Psalm 18:19).

This is what God intends for every one of His children when the enemy comes upon them like a flood. The Lord "prevents" them with His love. In other words, He comes to them saying, "I promise you are going to come out of this standing. You may be wounded, but that doesn't matter. I have already made you victorious." This sort of promise brings utter joy to the heart, and that joy makes us strong for the battle. We are lifted above our enemies, because we know our Lord has planted in us a sure word.

CLAIMING VICTORY

Because of the New Covenant, we are able to claim victory and dominion *even before the battle begins*. This is a blessing of the Davidic Covenant that God encompassed in the New.

God has promised us through the New Covenant: "I will subdue your enemies—your flesh, your temptations and the devil. You cannot overcome them on your own. You must trust in My covenant promises, and then you will be able to rejoice in victory even before you go to battle. You can claim your crown of dominion before the fight begins."

Suddenly, David was full of joy! He sang, "The king shall joy in Your strength, O LORD; and in Your salvation how greatly shall he rejoice! You have given him his heart's desire, and have not withheld the request of his lips" (Psalm 21:1–2). As you read this, you may wonder, "Why is David rejoicing? He's facing the most intense attack he has ever known. The enemy is bearing down on him with greater fury than ever, and he could be wounded or killed. How can he have such joy when he's facing such a powerful enemy?"

David answers this himself: "Thou preventest him with the blessings of goodness: thou settest a crown of pure gold on his head" (Psalm 21:3, KJV). What David is saying here is absolutely life-changing. Simply put, he tells us, "I face a powerful enemy who is bent on destroying me, but I am no longer afraid or troubled. Instead, I rejoice, because my soul is at peace. Why? The Lord has foreseen my struggle. He has already anticipated the enemy's strategy against me, and He has sent His heavenly forces ahead to do battle for me.

"My God has showered me with assurances of His love, and I know He isn't mad at me. I may be warring against an enemy who can cause me to stumble or fall, and at some point it may seem as though I'm finished. God has told me that if I will just get up, I will receive His strength and win the battle. He has given me the power of His very own Spirit."

David then made this statement of faith just before going to war: "Thou settest a crown of pure gold on [my] head" (Psalm 21:3, KJV). The crown of gold David mentions here is a symbol of victory and dominion. In short, David was absolutely confident he would defeat his enemies in battle. He was saying, "I'm going to war riding on God's promise to me. He said I would walk out of the battle wearing the crown of victory."

This is the doctrine of God's preventing goodness: He has anticipated all our struggles—all our battles with sin, flesh and the devil—and in His mercy and goodness, He has paid our debt before it can even come due. Through the covenant, He has prepaid for all our failures and relapses. His covenant oath assures us of His preventing goodness in our lives.

So, our victory is a done deal. Please understand, however, this doctrine does not apply to Christians who flirt with sin. By refusing to part with their lusts, they have already surrendered to the enemy. Such people simply do not want to be free, and they have already developed a hardened heart. They have tested God's grace and love again and again, until finally they have come to despise it.

God's preventing goodness applies only to those who love Jesus and have been surprised by sin. The Lord assures us that even if we are cast down temporarily, we will emerge from the battle standing upright—because Jesus has paid our debt. We are to trust Him, therefore, by laying hold of His promises. He will bring us out of the battle in His strength.

Perhaps you have been wounded and bloodied by the enemy's sword. You have failed in some way, and now you are downcast in spirit, wondering if you will ever recover. Do not lie there and die. Get up! You cannot continue to wallow in guilt, wondering, "Where did I go wrong?" Stand on the covenant promises of God's lovingkindness. Confess and lay hold of His forgiveness. He promised that you would come out of every battle a victor—crowned not by your own strength or ability, but by His. "Be exalted, O LORD, in Your own strength! We will sing and praise Your power" (Psalm 21:13).

A MATTER OF TRUST

How does the Lord prevent us with these blessings of goodness and lovingkindness? The Holy Spirit drives out all fear from us—fear of falling, fear of being cut off from God, fear of losing the presence of the Holy Spirit—by implanting in us His joy. We are to go forth rejoicing—exceedingly glad, as David was—because God has assured us we will prevail.

Yet so few Christians have this joy and exceeding gladness. Multitudes in the Church walk around as if they are in mourning—never knowing rest of soul or the peace of Christ's presence. They picture themselves under the thumb of God's wrath rather than under His protective wings. They see Him as a harsh taskmaster, always ready to bring a whip down on their backs, and so their lives are filled with fear, guilt and despair. They live unhappily, with no hope, more dead than alive.

In God's eyes, our problem is not sin, it is trust. Jesus settled our sin problem once and for all at Calvary. He does not constantly harp on us now, barking, "What have you done this time?" or "Now you've gone too far," or "This time you've crossed the line." No, never! Our Lord's attitude toward us is just the opposite. His Spirit is constantly wooing us, reminding us of the Father's lovingkindness—even in the midst of failure.

The real problem is our lack of faith in God's covenant promises. We refuse to accept His unconditional love, His unlimited forgiveness, His free reconciliation. We are not willing to believe He pardons and restores us simply because He loves us. Instead, we become focused on our sin, losing all sight of what God wants from us most. His Word says very clearly, "Without faith it is impossible to please Him, for he who comes to God must believe that He is, and that He is a rewarder of those who diligently seek Him" (Hebrews 11:6).

This verse says it all. Our God is a rewarder—and He is so anxious to shower us with His lovingkindness that He blesses us way ahead of schedule. It's almost as if He is too impatient to wait on our confession and prayers, so He rushes in and begins blessing us ahead of time. That is how much He loves us.

This is the concept our heavenly Father longs for us to have of Him. He is an all-seeing God, so He knows when our hearts are going to be repentant over our failures and sins. He knows when our contriteness and prayers are coming, but He cannot wait for the due date. He jumps in, saying, "I'm going to prevent My child with My blessings of goodness. I want to assure him he's not going to be judged, because I have already forgiven him through My Son's cleansing blood."

How God's Heart Rushes In

David serves as a great example of someone who was blessed with God's goodness even though he went "too far." You know his story. He went way beyond temptation, falling into blatant adultery, and then things got worse: David lied to cover his sin. When that did not work, he committed murder to keep from being found out. David became a hypocrite—sinning in the face of God's blessings, causing God's enemies to rejoice and bringing shame on the name of the Lord. Yet, we all know how the story ended. David was forgiven and fully restored, though he was disciplined severely.

My question is, At what point was David forgiven? God sent the prophet Nathan to confront David about his sin. The Lord said, "I want you to tell David how evil his sin is in My sight. And as a result of his iniquity, the sword will not depart from his house. The illegitimate baby he fathered with Bathsheba will die, and his wives will be ravished in the sight of all Israel." He then told Nathan, "Finally, tell David I have wiped out all his sins. He is no longer under judgment. I'm not going to kill him. Assure him he is totally forgiven."

Think about it—when God said this to Nathan, David was still in denial about his sin. He had not even confessed it yet. Do you see what was happening? God was forgiving this man before he had even faced his sin—before he could utter a prayer.

You see, God knows all—and he knew David's heart. He knew that when Nathan would confront him, David would blurt out, "Oh, Lord, I have sinned horribly. I'm so sorry for what I've done. I have carried this burden for an entire year, and I can't handle it anymore. Thank God, it has all been brought out into the open."

God knew David would be broken and contrite over his sin. Yet, most of all, the Lord knew that at heart David was not a habitual adulterer or murderer. Instead, David had been surprised by sin, overwhelmed by his lust. This man did not wake up one morning and decide, "Today I'm going to indulge my lust. I'm going up to my roof to peep around until I spy a nude woman bathing on her rooftop. Then I'll bring her here to the palace and seduce her." No—I am convinced lust moved in suddenly on David and overwhelmed him in a moment of weakness.

Likewise, God knows your heart. You may be trapped in bondage, having been overwhelmed by sin. But the Lord knows you did not wake up one day and decide, "Today I'm going out to commit fornication. I'm going to find a way to lose my temper and explode, cursing someone out. Then I'll download pornography, the raunchiest stuff I can find." No, only hardened souls behave this way—Gospel-rejecters, lovers of sin. Broken, contrite Christians do not plan to sin; they are surprised and overtaken by their lust. In fact, often the enemy comes in like a flood upon them while they are busy about God's business.

Beloved, God has counted your tears even before you have shed them. He has already forgiven you, at the point of your first pang of conviction and sorrow. He wiped away your sin just seconds after you committed it, when the awful pain struck your heart and you cried, "Oh, God, I hate this—I despise it. I'm so sorry I have grieved You." He knows you are not set on continuing in sin. He sees the tiniest flash of contriteness in your heart the moment it first appears.

God knew the pain David was facing, and He also knew that for the next several years David would go through severe discipline. He wanted to move in quickly with His comfort—He just could not wait. He said, "I've got to get to My servant to let him know that I know his heart, and that I've forgiven him." So God rushed in to prevent David with the blessings of His grace.

We see a picture of this when David brought Bathsheba into his house. After their illegitimate child died, God blessed them with another child—and this one He named *Jedidiah*, which

His covenant brings us into His loving arms and holds us tightly in the safety of His promise to us.

The church I grew up in in Southern California had lots of rules—you can do this, you can't do that—and I learned what was expected of me. I believed that the more I obeyed God, the happier He would be with me. The trouble was, no matter how hard I tried, I never felt that I really measured up.

I loved the Lord with all my heart and I believed He had a plan for me. I understood that the Holy Spirit dwelt in me and I received His presence with great expectation. But still I struggled. I sought to be the perfect daughter who would bring Him joy, and when I failed I wept. Had I let Him down? Was He disappointed with me? Even though I had loved Jesus since I was five years old, I felt that my best efforts to please Him were not good enough. I cried out to God for help on many occasions.

After I received David Wilkerson's teaching on the New Covenant, I began to understand that God is not nearly as interested in what I do as He is in my motivation. Jesus said, "If you love Me, keep My commandments" (John 14:15). I realized that I could never be "good enough" to make God happy. But I could love Him with my whole heart and He would receive my efforts to obey as my gift to Him—my love gift.

This change in the order of love and obedience has changed my life. I still struggle at times, of course, and I know I mess up. But now I know that loving Him is what makes me want to obey Him and that His Holy Spirit gives me power to stand against sin.

My new understanding has changed the way I teach. I no longer try to force people to act a certain way. I simply show them, with God's own words, how much He loves them and then I invite them to enter into that loving relationship with Him and love Him in return. I believe with all my heart that if we show His love and grace to those who so desperately need Him and are searching, they will respond and receive His love.

His covenant brings us into His loving arms and holds us tightly in the safety of His promise to us.

—Kim

means "God knows." The Lord was assuring David, "I know your heart—and I see your brokenness."

ONE FINAL EXAMPLE: THE PRODIGAL SON

I believe the Prodigal Son came home because of his history with his father. This young man knew his father's character—and apparently he had received great love from him. Otherwise, why would he return to a man who would have been angry and vengeful, one who would beat him and make him pay back every cent he squandered? He must have known that if he returned he would not be upbraided or condemned for his sins. He probably thought, *I know my father loves me. He won't throw my sin in my face. He will take me back.* When you have that kind of history, you can always go back home.

Notice how the Prodigal's father prevented him with the blessings of goodness. The young man was intent on offering a heartfelt confession to his dad, because Scripture tells us he rehearsed it all the way home. Yet when he faced his father, he did not get a chance to confess fully. His father interrupted him by running up to him and embracing him. The Bible says, "When he was still a great way off, his father saw him and had compassion, and ran and fell on his neck and kissed him" (Luke 15:20). The father was so happy his son was back, he covered him with kisses, saying, "I love you, my son. Come home with me now and be restored."

The Prodigal's father did all of this before his son could complete his confession. The young man was only able to blurt out the beginning of his speech, saying, "Father, I have sinned against heaven and in your sight, and am no longer worthy to be called your son" (Luke 15:21). But his dad did not wait for him to finish. To him, the young man's sin had already been settled. The father's only response was to issue an order to his servants: "Put a robe on my son and rings on his fingers. Prepare a feast, because we're going to celebrate. Everyone rejoice—my son is home!"

At what point was the Prodigal forgiven? He was forgiven back when he was still groveling for food in the pigpen. His sin was wiped away the moment he first thought, *I'm going back home. I've got to confess to my father that I've sinned.* He was forgiven by his father before he could even voice his confession—before he could do penance, weep tears of grief or try to pay him back. And his father showered him with blessings of goodness way ahead of schedule.

Sin was not the issue to this father. The only issue in his mind was love. He wanted his boy to know he was accepted, even before he could utter a confession. And that is the point God wants to make to us all: His love is greater than all of our sins. "The goodness of God leads you to repentance" (Romans 2:4).

Of course, it is possible to "despise the riches of His goodness, forbearance, and longsuffering, not knowing that the goodness of God leads you to repentance" (Romans 2:4). Those who think they can continue in sin, testing God's grace over and over, become hardened by their repetitious sinning. They believe they can continue to sin against His goodness without being harmed. But gradually, their hearts become impenitent, so that they no longer desire to repent. They end up with hardened hearts, storing up wrath against themselves. They cannot blame God; He has faithfully tried to prevent them with blessings of goodness—yet they have rejected it all. That is the greatest sin anyone can commit.

Here is the way to cleansing and restoration—by receiving the Lord's covenant promise. Hear these words: